NEVER *the* SAME

Reflections of a Baptist Minister Struggling Through the Loss of His Partner, Confidant, Best Friend, Critic and Loving Wife

DR. BILL MCENTIRE

WESTBOW
PRESS®
A DIVISION OF THOMAS NELSON
& ZONDERVAN

Copyright © 2017 Billy McEntire.

All rights reserved. No part of this book may be used or reproduced by any means, graphic, electronic, or mechanical, including photocopying, recording, taping or by any information storage retrieval system without the written permission of the author except in the case of brief quotations embodied in critical articles and reviews.

Scripture taken from the New King James Version®. Copyright © 1982 by Thomas Nelson. Used by permission. All rights reserved.

This book is a work of non-fiction. Unless otherwise noted, the author and the publisher make no explicit guarantees as to the accuracy of the information contained in this book and in some cases, names of people and places have been altered to protect their privacy.

WestBow Press books may be ordered through booksellers or by contacting:

WestBow Press
A Division of Thomas Nelson & Zondervan
1663 Liberty Drive
Bloomington, IN 47403
www.westbowpress.com
1 (866) 928-1240

Because of the dynamic nature of the Internet, any web addresses or links contained in this book may have changed since publication and may no longer be valid. The views expressed in this work are solely those of the author and do not necessarily reflect the views of the publisher, and the publisher hereby disclaims any responsibility for them.

Any people depicted in stock imagery provided by Thinkstock are models, and such images are being used for illustrative purposes only. Certain stock imagery © Thinkstock.

ISBN: 978-1-5127-7508-2 (sc)
ISBN: 978-1-5127-7509-9 (hc)
ISBN: 978-1-5127-7507-5 (e)

Library of Congress Control Number: 2017901823

Print information available on the last page.

WestBow Press rev. date: 02/16/2017

Contents

Dedication vii
Acknowledgments ix
Preface xiii

One Awesome Week 1
My Most Horrible Day 11
My Spiritual Family 21
Our Lonely Walk 34
I Only Said, "See You Later" 43
So Full, Yet So Empty 53
Stuck in the Middle 67
My Public Meltdown 76
God Loves Me: I Am Not Alone 85
Countless Struggles, God's Work Goes On 99

Dedication

This book is dedicated, first, to the glory of Almighty God, who has brought me to the point where I can function and live again productively. I give God the glory for allowing me to discover his Son, Jesus Christ, as the cleanser and forgiver of my soul. I belong to him. Second, I dedicate this book to the memory of my loving wife, Wanda Lynn Powell McEntire, who was such a wonderful encourager in the ministry, who continues to live in my heart, and who even now is celebrating with Jesus. And third, I dedicate this book to my family and church family who have accepted me and loved me throughout my journey.

Acknowledgments

I would like, first of all, to thank my Savior Jesus Christ for his love, forgiveness, and comfort. Without God in my life, I would hate to think what might have happened to me these last few months. I am constantly in a state of thankfulness to my creator, sustainer, master, and ultimate comforter in life. I can hardly wait to see him face-to-face. Our Holy Spirit is so comforting to us.

I also want to thank my dear family, who have supported me throughout my pain, sorrow, feeling of loss, and continual recovery. I especially want to thank my mother, Sara, mother-in-law, Phyllis, and sister, Judy, for their understanding and support through my emptiness and loneliness, which I struggle with each day. All my other family members, in their own way, helped me through my horrible loss. I am not alone; they also suffered a terrible loss.

Third, I want to thank my dear friends from Black Creek Baptist Church in Dovesville, South Carolina. You have been with me through the rough and tough times, and you have ministered to me far above and beyond the call of Christian friendship and service. Each of you has been my pastor, and I am eternally grateful for your ministry and love.

Fourth, I want to thank my pastor friends who have encouraged me in this first year of extraordinary change and loss. This segment of my life has not been easy, but God has kept me in the palm of His hand, and I am eternally grateful for that. I especially want to thank Rev. Tommy Gaskin, Rev. Sidney Calhoun, Rev. Eric Sloan, Rev. Dave Worthington, and Dr. Lisa Willard. You all are true friends and fellow laborers in the service of the Lord.

I have made friends from my four ministries, and I want to thank my special spiritual friends from Pleasant Grove Baptist Church (Aulander, North Carolina), Antioch Baptist Church (Red Oak, Virginia), and Clarksville, Virginia.

I also want to express my thanks for all those who have inspired me to write this book, which is so spiritually and personally emotional. I am so thankful for those who have been a part of my life in the thirty-plus years of ministry. God is so great to all of us, and I hope that this book will help others to keep on keeping on in the blessings of our Savior Jesus Christ through God's deep and abiding love. Living alone is a great struggle, but overcoming that hurdle can be accomplished by trust and assurance in Almighty God.

This book is about my struggle after I lost the love of my life, my wife, Wanda. Before we met, I prayed a great deal for God to send me the right woman. I met Wanda at Southeastern Baptist Theological Seminary in Wake Forest, North Carolina. What better place to meet your mate than on the chapel steps of a church? After dating for two years, we were married and began ministry together. One thing that you need to know is that we always put our Savior Jesus Christ first in our lives. Nothing was more important to us than Jesus. Today, Jesus remains the most important person in my life. I hope that this book helps people realize that there is an abundant and happy life after the loss of your mate. It never gets better, but each one of us learns to cope. Time does not heal, but God does.

The title, *Never the Same,* entered my heart after I lost my precious Wanda. This best describes my present day-to-day situation. I hope my struggles will give you some encouragement and help you to keep on keeping on. God continues to fill my life with his love and direction, but I continue to feel empty without my mate. God is all sufficient and heals us completely. I am so grateful to him for all he does for me. Without him, I am nothing.

I want to especially thank all of the people at Westbow Publishing for their encouragement, affirmation and direction during this special project. I appreciate everyone who enabled me to share my heart and soul with so many people. Thanks to all of you for your patience and understanding throughout these pages and this process.

Preface

When you endure a tragic event such as the death of a spouse, you are not alone. Countless millions of people are in the same boat, rowing together; they understand each other. For several days, perhaps weeks, I thought I was all alone. I had performed many funerals for church members over the years, and I thought I understood their spouses' feelings. Clearly, I did not understand, nor could I personally relate in that way. I was overwhelmed with the sense of loss in my own life. I thought that I was literally all alone and that everyone had abandoned me. My world had crumbled right before me. Very quickly, I realized that I was not alone; my Almighty God was holding me in His hands and embracing me in his arms. One could say that as a believer in Jesus Christ, God was literally carrying me through the loneliness and grief that had engulfed me. Praise God for that act of grace and mercy.

God is a comfort to us in his word. I immediately recalled Joshua 1:5b–6a, which says, "As I was with Moses, so shall I be with you. I will not leave you nor forsake you. Be strong and of good courage." Another scripture from Hebrews 13:5b says, "For He Himself has said, 'I will never leave you nor forsake you.'" This living scripture hit me in the pit of my stomach and in my heart as I was rushed out of the emergency room, where the doctors were working on my wife. God gives us grace for the moment and the hour. I am so thankful that God does this to those who trust and believe in Him and in His Son Jesus Christ.

Allow the people in your lives, who have experienced the same type of grief that you have encountered, to embrace you with love and understanding. You see, I had envisioned that Wanda and I would be rocking together on the front porch, sipping hot chocolate and drinking coffee in our final retirement years. Boy, that was blown out of the water. Wanda today is sipping the best of chocolate with Jesus in heaven. I am assured of that fact, and I know I will see her again soon, real soon. I am not alone. God continues to minister to my needs, and he will do the same for you, if you allow it. There is nothing like the embrace of God in the wee hours of the morning in one's loneliness. God is with you and me through this loneliness. He continues to sustain us through our lives, until he calls us to be with him.

If this book can help one person continue in their journey in life, it will be successful. I pray that God will minister to your needs as you read these very personal accounts of my struggles to continue in life amid my restructuring and remolding, by our master and King Jesus. Know this: Our master of the universe continues to carry you in your new life. May we all give God the credit for all he does. Let us all keep our eyes and minds upon Jesus. He is worthy to be glorified and praised. In actuality, when one spouse passes, another true reality sets in, and life is never the same, nor will it ever be the same. Nothing in this world hurts as much as losing your spouse. The hurt fades but never leaves the damaged heart.

Life now seems as if I am looking out of a door from a dark room, but the light of Jesus continues to get brighter and brighter each passing day. Through the awareness of God's love for me and his presence, I can see in that light that good things are awaiting me. I can begin to reflect upon past memories, and I find myself crying and laughing at the same time. That is good, real good. The pieces of life will come back together as I accept the things I cannot change. God is that constant force in our lives that helps us move forward. Tap into that force through the love of Jesus. He will never let you down.

Chapter 1

One Awesome Week

The demands of Wanda's human resource job at a local cleaning company near Florence, South Carolina, had taken its toll, and my wife needed a break. I had been working intently with some of the church members at Black Creek, and we both needed some downtime from our jobs. Although we called them our jobs, they were ministry opportunities. We always placed Jesus first in our work and relaxation. The people we served knew this and respected our commitments.

We had both worked long, hard hours and were looking forward to a beautiful, relaxing vacation week at Myrtle Beach, South Carolina. You see, each fall, for almost twenty years, we have gone on vacation to Land's End Resort at North Myrtle Beach. We had finally found a special place where we could unwind from the busy demands of work and just "be." Have you ever done that? Just "be"? Have you ever just kicked your gear shift out into neutral and idled for an entire week, doing nothing? For some time, Wanda had been very tired and under the care of a doctor at the Medical University of South Carolina at Charleston. Everything was going very well, and she was feeling good and looking forward to this vacation for some time—and I was too.

We both worked hard to save money to pay for the reservations. One day, I asked Wanda if her mother might like to come and vacation with us. She was also working hard in her custom framing shop in South Boston, Virginia. After a little persuasion, I was able to get Phyllis to consent to come down for a long-awaited and well-deserved vacation. She was thrilled to be coming to spend some time with us. Wanda and Phyllis often talked to each other three or four times each day. They had a wonderful mother-daughter relationship. She came on a Friday, and we set off to go to the condominium resort on Saturday, October 24, 2015. We had such a good trip traveling to our special resort. We talked and caught up on the news back home in Virginia. We laughed and had a remarkable trip to the beach that cool fall afternoon. We arrived earlier than we expected, and the room was ready for us. After a quick trip to the local Kroger grocery store, we settled in for the week of utter relaxation and rest, as we anticipated a quiet and peaceful time, with no expectations or demands from anyone. Ah, what a life, even for a week!

Now, one must understand that it is always very difficult to go on a vacation as a minister of a church. For many years, we have packed and loaded all our vacation paraphernalia in the car only to go back and answer the phone. *If I had only closed the door and ignored the phone!* But I cannot do that; I am called to serve our Lord and Savior, Jesus Christ. When the call would come, I would have to become available to the family that was in need. On the other end would be an emergency or a death. Well, you guessed it—we would not go on vacation. Once when we were planning for a different vacation, this happened for six weeks in a row, and finally I said we would just be sneaking off. After all the items were taken care of, we were able to get off on a trip to a wonderful vacation. It was a vacation for the record books, not soon to be forgotten. It was at a farmhouse in the fall in Beech Mountain, North Carolina. It was an awesome time with each other and with God.

If you are a minister, you can relate to what I just said. You know the disappointments of not being able to go on that well-deserved vacation or being called back for emergencies. After you deal with the situation, you may even be able to salvage a few days of that vacation. Sometimes this happens, but for us, it never did. But, as I said, I did not grumble or complain, for we were serving our awesome Savior and Lord, Jesus Christ, and I would do the same thing again. We had a very enjoyable time on that vacation in the North Carolina mountains that year.

Usually, we do not make long-range plans, but when it came to that vacation to Myrtle Beach, God had lined all this up—and we had a great time. No phone calls, no meetings, and no work to do at all. We enjoyed the entire week with food, books to read, places to see, and plenty of rest and relaxation. I very vividly remember that when we arrived in the condo, Wanda would turn up the heat and open the sliding-glass door to see the waves of the ocean. "Ah, what a life," she would exclaim. "How awesome is our God for all He has created." Wanda was so thrilled to see God's creation.

Wanda was feeling better just by looking at the ocean while the waves crashed as the tide came in and out. It seemed like she could let all her worries go out to sea and start over fresh each morning—or for each hour, for that matter. God was really wonderful to us while on this vacation. We really could sense his awesome presence in everything we did. At times, it seemed as if we could join in holding his hands as we looked at his wonderful creation around us. I could not put my finger on it or wrap my mind around it, but something seemed so much different than any other vacation that we had been on.

Little did I know that this would be our last vacation together. I love to sit and look at the ocean. It seems to soothe all our worries and cares. It is a time to think and reflect about life and about what God has done and what he will do in the future. I dismissed the thoughts and rejoined Wanda and Phyllis—and just let the good times roll.

Wanda loved to go places and ride around in the car. We did that as often as we could in life. She especially loved getting in the Jeep during the winter and sliding on the asphalt after a snowfall came the night before. She loved that and countless other things in life. She above all loved to sit on the beach and soak in the sun while listening to the crashing waves as she felt the breeze. If she had scales and fins, she would have made an outstanding fish. She truly loved the ocean. She also loved going to the mountains with me.

I remember when I took her home to meet my family. She looked at the mountain ahead of us and made the statement, "I wonder what it would be like to know someone who could show you around that mountain." I said, "Do you really want to see that mountain?" She very enthusiastically said, "Yes, I do!" So off I took her up a side dirt road toward Cedar Creek. She loved to see the various animals that we ran into (not with the car, mind you). We came upon a creek, and she asked me to stop. I did, and she took her shoes and socks off and had to sit on a rock with her feet in the water. Well, the mountain water was very cold, so much so that her toes turned blue. This was in July, and I found myself turning on the heater in the car to warm her little tootsies. We laughed about that very often. She had a ball in life and poured herself out as she shared Jesus. That was one trait that I loved about her so much.

While we were at the beach, we would have a ball. We would always take food or purchase it after arriving. We usually would eat breakfast and lunch at the condo, and later in the evening, we would go to Nance's at Murrells Inlet, Chestnut Hill, or the Chesapeake House at North Myrtle Beach and eat a delicious seafood supper. At times, the weather would not cooperate, and we would reverse our plans and eat lunch out, but for the most part, we would eat our evening meal out. Sometimes, we would venture up the beach to Calabash and eat at the Boundary House or at Ella's, which had delicious seafood. Occasionally, we would bite the bullet, as Wanda would say, and eat at the greasy Seafood Hut at Calabash. When you ate that food early in the day, you had time to work it off, and it would not choke your gizzard out during the night. The food was delicious, but the line would wind out the door and around the parking lot. Sometimes, you had to wait for about an hour, but it was worth it. Boy, we had many times like that. All of these precious memories were made along with delicious food to enjoy.

Do you see how we have a great time at the beach? We loved to eat and enjoyed doing it. When we would get tired of seafood, we would wind up at one of the Mexican, Italian, or American restaurants, which were also good. Now Phyllis, Wanda's mother, loved all this food, just as we did. At times, we would have a little skirmish over where to go eat. Usually, the womenfolk would win. I kind of liked it because they always picked a wonderful place to eat. It really did not matter to me, as long as we were together. What a blessing, to be together.

I really enjoyed this vacation. For the first few days, I would get up, watch the beautiful sunrise over the ocean, and have breakfast; I would then go to bed again and sleep until lunch, eat, and go back to bed, and then get up and eat supper—and then later go back to bed. Sounds like a lot of eating and sleeping, but that was my way of getting deprogrammed from the rut that we as ministers get in. Wanda and Phyllis would look at me, shake their heads, and laugh. Later on in the middle of the week, I would shake my head and laugh as they literally dragged me as their beast of burden to the local outlet mall for their annual shopping spree.

I would usually find a bench to sit down and meet other men whose wives were shopping. You know, there is always a "husbands' bench" around at shopping centers. We usually would strike up a great conversation, often discovering that we knew someone from the same town. I knew that I had better not disturb Wanda and Phyllis while shopping, so I would remain seated and meet other people or take in the scenery. They had a wonderful time while shopping that year. They both seemed to enjoy it as much as eating one of those great seafood suppers. What a memory to see them both smile and have a great time together.

Now, let me tell you something about South Carolina. Whether you are in the upstate, midlands, low country, or at the beach, there is nothing like watching the sunset in the western sky. I have seen more beautiful sunsets in South Carolina than anywhere in the world. It wasn't as pretty in South Africa, where we went on a mission trip, but was beautiful nonetheless. Wanda loved to see the sunsets. Oftentimes, we would pull off the road until the sun had completely gone down. It was unusually special after a storm. It would fill the sky with burnt-orange colors that would make you get goose bumps, thinking about God's creation. I shall never see a sunset again, like I did when I saw it with the love of my life.

Well, many people have partners to go into business with. But our life was a true partnership, and we did everything together. I mean everything together. One thing that Wanda did not really care to do is go to the grocery store. I loved it and made it fun. She often asked me to go to the store to get a certain item for her. If I could not find it, I would call her and ask her where it lived on the shelf. She always got a chuckle out of that. She could not spell all that well, either. Getting items from the grocery store was always a special event for both of us.

One day for Christmas, she sent me to get something she wrote on the shopping list. For the life of me, I could not decipher what she had written. I called her, and she asked me to spell it out. Here is what she spelled: "Press tiles." I asked her what in the world it was.

She said, "You know, those little twisty things that are brown with salt on them, only I want the small ones."

In an instant, I knew what she meant. "Pretzel" was the word; for a few weeks, I tried to get her to spell it. She still could not get it right. I loved her anyway, and I still dearly love her. Oh, how I miss the special little things that only she did. She was the greatest partner in life I could ever have. This old North Carolina boy had to travel to the cotton and tobacco fields of Virginia to find her. I would do it again and again for the wonderful memories we shared together.

Another trip to the grocery store was on a Memorial Day weekend. We had wanted some barbeque ribs but did not want to grill them because of the oppressive heat and humidity here in South Carolina. So we went to local grocery store, and there was a man grilling some mouth-watering ribs. We purchased a rack of these beautiful ribs. Now we wanted to make sure that they had plenty of sauce with them. We began to open them in that thick hard plastic that they put them in. Well, we pulled, snapped, and tugged so much that we all of a sudden found the ribs flying out of the plastic container and on us, the grocery cart, and onto the floor. We both stood there and laughed until we cried; needless to say, we needed no sauce for our ribs. The deli cashier saw what happened and gave us another rack of ribs. We ate them and laughed countless times about that trip to the grocery store.

We were partners in ministry; we praised God together, prayed together, and read the Bible together. We both allowed Jesus to take first place in our lives. We were sold out to our Savior and Lord of our lives. One could say that we both surrendered to Jesus as our maker and keeper of our souls. We oftentimes would discuss the deep, deep things of God and would always find time to pray for one of the children's goldfish that was sick. A matter of fact, we prayed for all of the children's special requests for the cat, dog, bat, or old bird that one of them had.

One day, one of the children wanted us to pray for an old crow near the house. The child said that it was hurt. We prayed, but later, we found out that the child was talking about the next-door neighbor, whose name happened to be Mrs. Crow. We laughed and laughed, but Mrs. Crow got better very soon.

Day after day went by at the beach, and we continued to love and enjoy our time together. Saturday through Wednesday always goes by at a snail's pace, but the rest of the week goes by like a roller coaster. Quickly, in a flash, it was gone. You cannot believe that over half the week was gone. Well, we tried to make the best of the week. Several mornings, I woke up early and took pictures of the sun coming up. Most of the time, it was peeking through the clouds, but beautiful nonetheless. As I said earlier, there is nothing like a South Carolina sunset.

Some of the things I will miss about our final vacation at the beach are too painful to restate. Most of all, I will miss seeing Wanda and her mother, laughing and picking at each other.

On Friday of that week, Wanda received a call from work. Her assistant asked how things were going.

Wanda said, "I have just finished spending the most fabulous vacation week of my life with my mother and the love of my life, Bill."

I have those words to hold onto. I have those words to help me through each day. I have the sound of that precious wife of mine who so lovingly said these words from the bottom of her heart. I continue to cherish the love I have with her. Just because she is out of my sight, I will never forget her, and I will never find anyone to replace her. You see, when I asked God for a woman I could love and be happy with, God gave me Wanda. I told God that I would never ask him for another woman if he gave me the right one to begin with. God always answers our prayers.

On Saturday, we woke up and started getting ready to leave. It was only about an hour and a half to North Myrtle Beach. Wanda was feeling a little sickly and was having trouble breathing. She thought she only had a stuffed-up nose and it would start draining soon. She had even more trouble getting to the vehicle to go home. She said very few words on our trip back to Dovesville, near Darlington. A matter of fact, none of us talked much. We finally arrived back home, and Wanda was feeling a little better. She was able to eat supper and was laughing some as we talked about how we enjoyed the vacation. Later that evening, her breathing got worse. Then she got much better and made it through the night. Phyllis and I were confused about what to do. We listened to God and followed his directions. I continued to have strange feelings deep within me. I could not even fathom the fact of losing Wanda. What about our golden years? What about the countless sunsets awaiting us?

I had a million things flooding through my mind and heart. What if I lost Wanda? What would I do? I was numb, confused, and empty, and I felt like life had ended as I knew it. I knew that it had not, but it sure did seem like it did. Unbelief, hurt, pain, and despair all hit me at once. I knew the stages of grief and felt like I was in all of them at the same time. It hurt! It really hurt so badly. I did not know if I could go on in life without Wanda or that I even wanted to. Before all that was to come God again gave me assurance and peace when I finally laid down for a little rest. I cannot remember if I ever went to sleep. I continued to feel like I was in a thick, choking fog and could not get out. I longed to see the bright sunshine and see Wanda's smiling face. I knew that I would not see her as she was before all this happened. I know that I must go on and make the best of my calling to serve God, even though it would be painful. I know that God will help me through all of this in his time. Only God knew what was going to transpire, and I left this all up to him.

Chapter 2

My Most Horrible Day

I had gone on to church to open the doors early that morning. It was November 1, 2015, Homecoming at Black Creek Baptist Church. Phyllis came on to worship services and went back to stay with Wanda. I finished up at church and went for a brief time to the fellowship hall and greeted people. God seemed to be telling me to go home.

When I exited the fellowship hall, I placed my hand on the doorknob, and on the other side was Phyllis, saying, "We have got to get Wanda to the hospital."

She could not even get up and walk. She was gasping for breath so bad that I began to get really worried, almost hysterical. Many questions went through our minds. I had called 911, which I have never done before, and I stumbled over our address but finally got it out. I waited impatiently but the ambulance finally arrived. We got her into the ambulance and followed it to McLeod Hospital.

My attention went straight to Wanda. I could not do anything except think of all the great times we had together in life. I tried to keep up with the ambulance, but it hurried ahead. In all respects, this was turning out to be the most horrible day of my life. I mean the most horrible day I have ever tried to live through. To this day, I hate to see an ambulance approaching my direction. I cannot even look at that "box of death on wheels" without tearing up and thinking of my wonderful Wanda. Finally, after what seemed like a lifetime, Phyllis and I arrived at McLeod Hospital. I helped my rock of a mother-in-law find a seat and ran to see where Wanda was. Before I continue, I need to let you know that Phyllis never treated me like a son-in-law. She always treated me as a son.

Many scenarios crossed my mind; I was falling victim to a lot of "what ifs," and I do not like to live that way. These ideas and situations kept entering my mind, and I finally did what I always tell people I minister to: I began to pray, and God gave me the greatest peace that I have ever known. God always comes through for us, even in the worst of situations. God always works his best through our worst in life. For the first time in a long time, I was feeling lost and undone, wondering what to do and which way to turn. Thank God for his peace and guidance.

Many other church family members had arrived, and the little private waiting room was almost full. If I ever had any doubts about how the people at Black Creek Church felt about me, they were dispelled through their presence. Time went on so slowly. My mind and heart wondered about so many things in life. It was as if I was in a deep thick fog and could not see the light of day. People prayed, and Phyllis and I continued to hold each other's hands; we sat impatiently waiting to hear about Wanda's condition.

My church family all rallied around us and prayed for our care and peace. Later, others came to the waiting room and offered their sympathy, and I found myself as a recipient of God's amazing strength and grace. I do not even deserve those gifts from God. I entered the room and was disheartened. Wanda was gasping so hard for breath. I wanted to breathe for her, but all that I tried did nothing to seem to ease the situation. The best way to describe her breathing was this way: Have you ever seen a dog panting hard after chasing a deer? That was the way Wanda was breathing, and it hurt me so much. I was able to get her to relax some, but her breathing only got worse and worse. I was helpless, useless, and I felt like my hands were tied so tight that I could not even swallow. The wonderful staff at the hospital told me to go find a seat; they needed to try to calm her down and work with her breathing.

So I went back to that cold dungeon of a place called the waiting room. I immediately saw one of the deacons at the church, Rufus Cribb, and his wife, Priscilla. They hung in with us all day long. They seemed to calm my nerves and comforted us as best they could. We would pray, talk, and pray some more. I went back and forth to Wanda's room, and I tried to comfort her as best I could. I told her I loved her, and we talked very briefly about the love and presence of God. I stayed with Wanda as long as I could, while the nurses constantly came in and out of the room. I thought that I was in the way, and they finally told me to go rest in the waiting room for a few minutes. I very reluctantly and slowly went back to the waiting room. Christian friends are the best people to have around in a crisis situation. I continue to thank God for each of them so much.

By this time, more people came to the hospital, and a crowd was beginning to form. Bobby and Sylvia Byrd came and offered great spiritual and moral support. We talked about a lot of things, as well as the homecoming and the visitors who were there.

They asked how Wanda was, and I said, "Not good at all." I went back to see how she was doing. Each time I went to see my dear wife, I found Wanda breathing even more sporadically and heavier. I felt horrible and useless. I only saw her slipping away from me, and we had so much more to do in life for the Lord. If only I could do something.

Wanda looked up and asked me for help. I told her whatever I could do, I would do it. Neither of us ever wanted to be put on a ventilator, but she begged me to help her decide what to do. I told her if that was what it would take to help her breathe better, we needed to do that. She wanted to breathe. She wanted so badly to tell her mother how much she loved her. I was trembling inside myself. I was a wreck, and I felt all alone. The nurse said if they did not put her on a ventilator, she was going to code. I could not bear that news. Ministering in the hospital as I did many times, I knew what that meant. This was very, very serious. I was on the verge of losing my loving wife, partner, and best friend.

I held Wanda by the hand, kissed her, and told her how much I loved her. I told her what a wonderful life we have had together, and she agreed. I kissed her and told her I loved her again.

She said that she loved me, paused, and added, "Bill, take care of yourself."

I promised her that I would. I told her that I was going back out into the waiting room to sit with her mother until they helped her breathe better. She said okay. I began to walk ever so slowly; everyone could see the pain and hurt on my face. I kept them all in the loop and said that we needed to pray and pray very hard, which is what we did.

By now, there were about thirty people from our church sitting with us, and it was a very somber mood. One of the deacons, Rick Young, said, "Preacher, it's all good," which was a normal saying of his.

At that time, I could have decked him, but I didn't. I knew he meant well, but at that time, nothing was good for me and my family. I was in pain and agony, and I was about to lose my dear wife.

Many other conversations went on, and I finally broke free to go into Wanda's room. She was breathing fine on the ventilator, and she looked at ease and so peaceful. I looked at the monitors over her head, and all of them were in a normal rhythm. I was feeling a little better. Hopefully, and prayerfully, God would perform a miracle for Wanda and me. I held Wanda's hand, kissed her on the lips, and said, "Wanda, if Jesus is reaching out to you, take Him by the hands and go be with Him."

Immediately, all the monitors that were normal went flat line. The nurses came running in and said she was coding. They pushed me out of the room, and I fell back against the wall. I closed my eyes and saw the gates of heaven being opened for Wanda to go through. I felt abundant peace and, at the same time, exhausting grief. You can believe it or not, but I know what I saw, even though my eyes were closed. God knew what I needed to get through, and he always delivers to his people. I knew that God was giving me confirmation of peace; as Deacon Young said, "It's all good." God is our awesome loving God who carries us through all things.

My mind immediately went to one of the scriptures I use at funerals; Revelations 21:4 states, "And God will wipe away every tear from their eyes; there shall be no more death, nor sorrow, nor crying. There shall be no more pain, for the former things have passed away." This gave me great comfort. God always helps us recall scripture when it is really needed.

I also recalled the scripture from 2 Corinthians 5:7–8, where Paul states, "For we walk by faith, not by sight. We are confident, yes, well pleased rather to be absent from the body and to be present with the Lord." I was horrified as to what the doctor might come and tell us in a few minutes. At the same time, I knew that God would give us grace to make it through.

I went out into the waiting room, and a nurse followed me and said, "I believe you all need to come with me into another waiting room."

I told everyone what had happened and said that the doctors and nurses were working on Wanda. By now, it was four in the afternoon, and I was so tired and frustrated, as well as hungry, but I could not eat a bite. Now this little waiting room had about forty people, including all of the deacons from Black Creek Church. One by one, they came and wrapped their arms around me with astounding comfort. I was on the other side of the table, for once in my life. I received their ministry with openness and great love. Forty ministers of the church were in the room with Phyllis and me. No matter what they said, it still hurt. It hurt deeply to the core of my existence. I was empty, so very empty.

I recall a very special person, Betty June Gandy, who ministered to me in an unusual way. She came and gently caressed my face, as a mother would, for about ten minutes. Oh, the comfort that she gave was overwhelming. I knew that she loved me more than a parishioner to the preacher. It was if God had sent an angel to me. It is a blessed event to have friends of all ages in the kingdom of Christ.

Finally, we heard the door behind us open, and I drew up as if I were a piece of bacon in a frying pan. I had hoped and prayed for hopeful news, but I knew it was not going to be good. A young doctor ever so slowly got on his knees, and it seemed like it took him forever to make eye contact. I knew what he was going to say, but somehow deep in my being, I did not want to hear it.

These were his words: "Mr. McEntire, I am sorry; we did all we could, but we could not bring your wife back."

My insides were yelling, and I had many feelings flood my soul.

One of the deacons told me that I looked at the doctor and said this: "Doctor, if you don't have Jesus in your heart and soul, you need to make that decision real soon." I do not even remember saying that, much less thinking that.

My real feelings were this: I felt like the devil was standing right in front of me and stuck his slimy hot arm in my mouth, down my throat, and ripped out my heart and my future. I immediately knew he did not because God takes care of his own people. I was in deep, deep pain, like I have never experienced before in my life. I immediately prayed for God to give me, Phyllis, and the entire family his abundant peace and assurance. God did that for us.

I had called my other family members and told them that Wanda was not doing well. Now, I had to call them back and tell them that she was gone to heaven. I called J. R., Wanda's brother, and his wife, Mickie, who were on their way back home to Virginia after visiting their daughter Amanda. I hated to tell them this news. They naturally pulled over on the side of the road. Wanda and J. R. were very close to each other. My sister, Judy, and my mother were on the way to the hospital, and I also told them the horrible news. As you could imagine, they too were shocked. They were in utter disbelief.

I will truly miss Wanda, my prayer partner and closest friend in life. I will never forget her. Some people say that you will get over it, but that is a bunch of bologna. God helps fill in the emptiness, the holes in your heart, and the loneliness of the long nights. We have seen prayers answered even before we got them out of our mouth. Whenever that happened, we would praise God for his wonderful answered prayers. You should always take time to thank your partner in ministry, in business, or spouse. And do it quickly, do not wait; you may not have another opportunity to do so. Cherish your partner in life and work out all your differences, if you have any. Wanda and I had plenty of differences, if you want to call them that. We always ironed them out before going to bed each night. Things sure were better after that. You will be glad you ironed those problems out, I can assure you of that.

Wanda was my dearest and best friend. I could share anything with her. And as women do, they processed everything out, and she helped me a great deal. She was a great critic and support in ministry. At times, she wondered if we would have to pack the moving van, but usually we did not. God always took care of the hard sermons. She gave me some great constructive criticism, which helped me become a better minister and servant of God. We complemented each other in that respect.

Yes, she was the love of my life. I will never have another love. When she looked at me, love would ooze out of her beautiful eyes. I still love her today and always will. I still miss her touch, her kiss, and her hands that lovingly cooked meals for me. I miss holding her hand as we walked along the beach or walked up a trail in the mountains.

I will miss her gentle touch as she caressed my sunburned face. I will miss hearing her hum songs of faith as she cooked our food or baked for someone in need. I will miss her warm, loving, forgiving smile that went to the very depths of her soul and back again. I will miss her funny spellings and thrilling times at the grocery store. I will never see Wanda, the love of my life, in this life again. I do have the assurance that I will see her again in heaven. I am looking forward to that moment.

As I look over my life, I can truly say that this was the most horrible day I ever had. I have had bad days and situations that were difficult, but never a day like this. Those other situations worked themselves out, or I reasonably talked over the issues with other people. I had all these thoughts within me, but I did not know where to start. I suppose that the beginning is a good place to start.

After we left the hospital, Phyllis and I just wanted to go home. The ride back to the parsonage seemed even longer. When we arrived, there were people standing outside in the rain, waiting for us. A pastor friend, Rev. Frankie Tanner, was waiting to minister to us. He grabbed me, wrapped his arms around me, and began to cry with me. He prayed and stayed for a while. Others were there talking or asking questions. By this time, other family members had arrived, and we were trying to muddle through; everything seemed to slap us in the face, unexpectedly.

Another pastor friend, Rev. Eric Sloan, who had lost his wife about a year earlier, came and talked and prayed with us. He knew exactly what I was feeling, and that was a great comfort to me. Finally, one of my dearest and best friends in ministry came and prayed with me. Rev. Tommy Gaskin stayed with us many times during the next four days. He continues to minister to me to this day. I value Tommy's friendship; he is a wonderful man of God. Mt. Olivet is truly blessed to have him and his wife, Frances.

Various family members began to arrive, and we sat down and began to talk. We could not believe all this was happening. Wanda and I had always talked about being together when Jesus came back again. I never thought she would be going on before me. I had the comfort that she was breathing so well. She had only begun to live with Jesus in heaven.

The hour was getting late; it was nearly midnight, and we

were so tired that we could not sleep. This was a bad feeling, but we tried to get some rest from the long day and for the long day ahead. Life throws so many unexpected things at us, but this was unbelievable and so hard to accept. Death will come to everyone, but this seemed so premature in our lives right now. God only knows, and he makes no mistakes at all. I am happy that Wanda knew Jesus, and she is with him now.

Chapter 3

My Spiritual Family

I could not have had a better congregation to support me and pray for me during all this confusion and loss. They loved me as their pastor, and I knew that each day of ministry with them was a blessing. They would express thanks for me being their pastor many times each week. Every October, they would have a gift of appreciation for me; usually it was a food gift card. Earlier, I told you how much I enjoyed eating and especially eating great food. Each Christmas, they would give me food certificates as gifts, and I always made them last into mid July. My people are wonderful to me, and I tell them as often as I can. As much as I love them, Jesus loves them more.

I have always been told that church people should be laborers together, and it is true. In 1 Corinthians 3:9, the word of God says, "For we are God's fellow workers." People at Black Creek and others have helped me so much, and I could not thank them enough. The only way I really could help them is to do what we are instructed to do in 1 Thessalonians 1:2, which says, "We give thanks to God always for you all, making mention of you in our prayers." I pray each day for my flock of lambs, whether they attend church or not. They are all special to me and are more special to God. I continue to have a special call here to serve God and these people. There have been some potholes and struggles, but God has continued to use us and love all of us.

If you do not have a church home and people who love you, then you are missing a great blessing. If you do have a church home but do not attend, then get back to church. There is no excuse for staying away from the family of God, so lay it all down at the feet of Jesus and let him take care of it. I hope you can value the people in your congregation and really love them. Do you really realize how important the people in your church are to you? Someone in your church will pray for you each day. Get in church; do not wait until the funeral director rolls you down the front in a fancy box. Go and get involved while you are living. Bury the hatchet, axe, or shovel, and put away those grudges, and forgive as Jesus forgives you. Your life will be better. Your spiritual health will also be better; it will begin to thrive.

Sorry, I had to do a little preaching, and I hope you take heed to those words I just stated. I am so blessed at Black Creek Church, and I thank God each day for these people. Some of them are more spiritual than others and enjoy talking about the deep truths of God. My spiritual family goes beyond the church where I am pastor. It goes back thirty-nine years.

I remember the spiritual guidance I received from a pastor friend of mine before attending college and seminary. When I answered the call to preach, Rev. Carrell Pruette told me that if I could be happy doing anything else, then I should do it. I did not understand what he meant, but after all these years, I know now what he was talking about. I am happy, and it is a pleasure to serve our living, saving God, through Jesus Christ. I would not change a thing in my service to our Lord.

There are many spiritual giants in my life, and I am thankful to God for using each one of them to encourage me along the way. Wanda was one of my greatest spiritual giants. She had the sweetest spirit about her. She loved reading so much. She often read three to five books each month, but the book she loved the most was the Bible. She would share her thoughts about a scripture, and we would discuss it until the wee hours of the morning. She embodied the love of Jesus not only at home, but at church, work, and anywhere we would go. She was like Coca-Cola; she was the real thing. She often hummed great songs of faith while she baked in the kitchen. She loved baking food and having me run all around the community delivering her cakes, pies, cookies, and breads. I enjoyed taking those baked goods to the people, and it always seemed to cheer them up so much.

Many times, we would sit on the back porch and talk about the wind and how it was like the Holy Spirit. In Acts 2:2, the wind is described like this: "And suddenly there came a sound from heaven as of a rushing mighty wind." How she longed and prayed for the Holy Spirit to take hold of more people. If everyone would obey the Holy Spirit, like the rushing mighty wind, we could win people to Jesus even faster and perhaps be in heaven at this very moment. I fear the wind during storms and the destruction it can bring. But the Holy Spirit does not bring on destruction; he brings on growth and building the kingdom of Christ.

I am reminded of another great passage in the Bible; Isaiah 43:1–3a states:

> But now, thus says the LORD, who created you, O Jacob, And He who formed you, O Israel: Fear not, for I have redeemed you; I have called *you* by your name; You *are* Mine. When you pass through the waters, I *will be* with

you; And through the rivers, they shall not overflow you. When you walk through the fire, you shall not be burned, Nor shall the flame scorch you. For I *am* the LORD your God, The Holy One of Israel, your Savior.

This is a real comfort for me right now in my life. I praise God for his comfort and the peace that he gives through his word. The word of God changes each of us and supplies for us all that we need when we only listen, follow, and apply it to our lives.

At times, I feel like I am without hope, but I know that Jesus is my living assurance. I will continue to surrender to him, for I know that he will never let me down, nor will he leave me. I feel him in everything I do, and I give Jesus the praise and glory for each new day. I cannot live without my loving Savior Jesus leading me and guiding me in the tasks that I must do for him each day. That gives me hope, peace of mind, and a new perspective each morning.

I feel like the water has thrust me out to sea, that the torrents have pushed and pulled me in every direction that one could imagine, but yet I am still here. I feel like the fire has consumed me at times, and I cannot breathe for the heat and smoke. Yet I am not scorched by the flames of Satan. The fire that tries to engulf the body dispels all my dreams for the future. I feel like I am choking and cannot get a deep, clean, clear breath. And finally, after all these feelings, and many more, I wake up again. I can see that there is going to be another day, yet one without my precious Wanda. I continue to struggle with many things that I now must do alone. In all those things I go through, I re-experience the fact that God is always with me. I cannot imagine not having him in my life. I would be ultimately destitute without God.

My spiritual family always comes through for me. Every time I get blue, am depressed, or feel low, something great happens. There are times when I need a phone call, and it always seems to be the right call from the right person. Then when the mail comes, I always get a note of encouragement and a blessing with a prayer. And then, there is a special visit when it is needed. God always knows what I need, when I need it. I am always amazed at how he knows those things, and he meets all my needs. I should not be amazed but I am, and I am in awe of the great love my Savior and Lord has for me. His protection is real and lasting.

It is downright comical when you see how God uses the scriptures through other people.

I found great strength in 2 Corinthians 1:3–4, which says, "Blessed be the God and Father of our Lord Jesus Christ, the Father of mercies and God of all comfort, who comforts us in all our tribulation, that we may be able to comfort those who are in any trouble, with the comfort with which we ourselves are comforted by God." Many of the widows in Black Creek Church were a great encouragement and inspiration to me through all my heartache and loss. I will now be able to do the same for others when I am called upon. There are so many blessings God has bestowed upon me, and many came through my church members. I have been told stories of others who have lost their spouse. Some of those people have been alone now for years, and others for just a short time. One aspect is that those who have gone on before are safe in the arms of our Savior Jesus Christ. Amen.

We have many widows in our church and a few widowers. One very special person, Amelia Smith, came to my office one Sunday morning and asked, "Preacher, are you going to be home this Tuesday?"

I said yes, and she had another odd question, I thought. She asked, "Are you going to be by yourself? I do not want to share you with anyone when I come."

I said yes, I would be at home alone. I asked her if she liked coffee and cookies. She said yes. I made some fresh coffee and made a few cookies. After she arrived, we began talking about life and marriage. Amelia was a big help in my grief recovery. She continues to be a wonderful counselor and friend, who listens to me and cries with me. I am thankful to God for her gentle understanding and encouragement. She continues to come by my office and talks to me, especially when she knows I am having a difficult time. Through the years, she has often invited me to her home to eat Sunday lunch with all her family. I really enjoy the advice and wisdom that she offers. She is a true loving Christian woman. You might say she's a rare gem.

Three other ladies in the church helped me a great deal: Frances Gleason, Frances Pearman, and Rae Kirven. All of us have lost our spouses and are struggling each day. I truly value the song, "One Day at a Time," more than I ever have. This is all we have. One day, and we must make the best of it. Those three ladies and I shared stories of our spouses, and we laugh, cry, pray, and help each other in life. It is wonderful to have someone who understands and has been through what you have gone through. I value their friendship so much more since we have so many more things in common.

Another great encouragement is my special friend, Deacon Otis Lawhon, our music minister. He is a caring person and has a tender heart. Wanda and I both loved how Otis directed the choir, and we witnessed his Christian life being so full of love and understanding. He loves the Lord and serves him whenever he has the opportunity. I am overwhelmed at times, and Otis always has a funny gesture or saying that helps me cheer up and continue. He is a true Christian brother who is genuine in faith.

Otis not only possesses the gift of singing, he has the gifts of discernment, understanding, surrender to the Lord, and teaching; he is also very encouraging. Otis can preach, and he has done so on several occasions. I am blessed to be able to call him one of my best friends. I hope we will always be able to stay in touch throughout life. We often go out to eat after church on Sunday or after going to hear a gospel group sing. He is truly a blessed man and has a great voice to glorify God. I appreciate him so much; he is real radical, active Christian. He genuinely loves his Lord and Savior Jesus Christ.

Hope is a precious commodity, especially Christian hope because we know that this hope is all the reassurance that Christ gives us. In Romans 15:4, these words give me a great deal of hope: "For whatever things were written before were written for our learning, that we through the patience and comfort of Scriptures might have hope." That hope is living inside of me and is nestled deep within my soul. Without this hope of Christ found in the scriptures, I would be a ship without a rudder, with no place to go. I am thankful to my Savior and God for the indwelling power and direction of the Holy Spirit, and for allowing me to possess the strength to continue. On cloudy and dreary days, I feel so depressed, but I feel my Savior within my heart, and I take another step or two and praise God in the process.

I would be remiss if I did not tell you how Dianne Todd has helped me during my continuing struggles. When I first came to Black Creek, I was hoping that the administrative assistant would not be a little old lady with a bun on her head, set in her ways. Well, at the same time, Dianne was hoping that I would not be a stuffed shirt: traditional, religious, historical, and a legalistic know-it-all. To say the least, God gave us both what we asked for. I received a nice spiritual person to speak to theologically, and she received a relaxed down-to-earth pastor. We both won, don't you think?

Dianne goes to an interdenominational church, and I find that refreshing. It is not unusual for the assistant to not attend the church. We have talked about every issue in the world. We have prayed about the situations of people and claimed healing for them. We have been able to encourage each other in the faith and share our own special journeys. Dianne loved Wanda because they were sisters in the Lord. She as well as others in the church continue to go through some form of grief over the loss of Wanda. We often talk about our lives before coming to Black Creek, and Dianne is amazed as to how God has led us to this position. Dianne is a biblical counselor, prayer warrior, listener, and most of all a true Christian representative for Christ. We love to talk about the things of God and know that he has many blessings waiting for Black Creek Church.

During our conversations, after talking about the goodness of God, we often lost track of time and had to hurry back to work. When she gets an inspirational thought or revelation, we stop and talk. Several times, Wanda would send over a piece of cake, pie, cookies, or muffins for Dianne to try. Whenever I let Wanda know that Dianne gobbled up the treats that she sent, I would witness the sweetest and most enormous smile come over her face. Cooking and baking gave her a great deal of pleasure. I sure do miss that helpmate and best friend of mine. I continue to cherish her down deep within my heart. I will never forget her and look forward to seeing her again in heaven.

One Friday night, Billy and Harriett Mahn invited Wanda and me to supper. Friday night was usually our night, but we talked it over and said, "Why not?" So for many Friday nights, we ate supper together. I thought it would end when Wanda went to be with the Lord, but they wanted to continue, and we minister to each other every Friday. It has been a time to remember Wanda and recall how special she still is to us.

By the same token, one Wednesday, Rufus Cribb invited me out to eat lunch. He saw this as a ministry opportunity to his pastor. It sure was and continues to be so. Now he pays one week, and the next week I pay. We have a great time together, as we discuss politics, religion, and world events. No one likes to eat by themselves. I welcome this midweek time. It is like a little oasis in the middle of Darlington at Sweet Jane's Restaurant. The food is great, and the atmosphere is wonderful. It reminds me of a time when Wanda and I went to Richmond, Virginia, to a Baptist convention and ate at a little bistro in the city. It was a charming and very vibrant place to visit.

There are so many people who have helped me through my grief and readjustment. I wonder if I will ever get through the grief process. The main aspect is that these people here love this old preacher boy, and I love them equally. The children keep me on my toes, and they are so loving. When I am down and out, the children always do something for me or come by the office and cheer me up. I am so blessed, and I know that I am where I am supposed to be. It gives me great pleasure and happiness, for God has placed me here for such a time as this. God knew what was going to occur when we moved here, and it blows my mind that only these people at Black Creek could have ministered to me as they have.

As I have been stating all along, I receive blessings from God's word, and I would like to share a scripture that has helped me a great deal to adjust to my situation. It is found in Psalm 142:1-7.

> I cry out to the LORD with my voice; With my voice to the LORD I make my supplication. I pour out my complaint before Him; I declare before Him my trouble. When my spirit was overwhelmed within me, Then You knew my path. In the way in which I walk They have secretly set a snare for me. Look on *my* right hand and see, For *there is* no one who acknowledges me; Refuge has failed me; No one cares for my soul. I cried out to You, O LORD: I said, "You *are* my refuge, My portion in the land of the living. Attend to my cry, For I am brought very low; Deliver me from my persecutors, For they are stronger than I. Bring my soul out of prison, That I may praise Your name; The righteous shall surround me, For You shall deal bountifully with me."

If you go back and reread verse 3, you will find the word "then." After I poured my heartache and grief to God, then he knew the new path I was to travel down. I may have not liked this new path, but I am getting used to the idea, and I struggle each day to go farther down the path. I am assured that as I travel down this path, even in my overwhelmed life, I know Christ holds my hand and had often carried me along the way. This psalm has been a blessing to me, and it is true; all that is described has been seen in my life these past few months. God is my refuge, he has brought me out of prison (so to speak), and I will always praise his name.

There is a benevolent group of people in our church, headed up by Marie Ross. These people provide food to those who have experienced a death in their family. Kathie Benton, Sylvia Byrd, Harriett Mahn, and many other women brought food to my kitchen and warmed it for my family to eat, and it continued for about a month. These people at Black Creek, especially the women, are spectacular.

My spiritual family has been here for me when I need them most. The deacons told me to take a few weeks off after the funeral, but I could not. You see, the more I threw myself into the ministry, the more I could get on with my life. When I was blue about life before all this nightmare happened, I often visited people. It seemed like helping others helped me get my perspective in life. It was a balm of healing for my soul to know that I could help others. We pastors are so geared to ministering to others that it is difficult for us to switch gears and become gracious recipients from our church members. It brings a great feeling to receive the soothing words and actions from my church family. In Galatians 6:2, we are told to "bear one another's burdens, and so fulfill the law of Christ." My loving Black Creek Church family have been here to help me bear the burden of being alone and dealing with sorrow; they give encouragement, understanding, and unending love. I am eternally grateful to all of them for all they do to help me get back on track.

The younger women of the church had a great relationship with Wanda. They, along with the entire church, grieved with me and are continuing with the struggles of filling in the empty spaces that Wanda left. Many pastors' wives do not feel that they are supposed to get involved with the church as Wanda did. Since she loved Jesus so much, and served him, she also had a call to work with the children and the mothers of those children. Wanda invested a great deal of time with all the children that we have ministered to over the past thirty years. Each one of those children have grown and learned about Jesus in a unique way. Some of them have given their lives and hearts to Jesus and are serving him on the mission fields in various ministries. All I can say is thank God for those women who have encouraged me on in our church. Even their children are concerned and pray for their hurting pastor.

Many times, Wanda would come back from supper or from a night out with the girls and would pray for each one of them individually. She loved being a part of their lives. She enjoyed going to the movies with them, to Cici's Pizza, shopping, or to the beach, or hanging out in the Children in Action department. I know that our younger ladies will miss Wanda, as I do.

James Howle was a young father who was really impressed and touched by Wanda. The day after Wanda went to be with the Lord, he found it difficult to come into the parsonage and visit with me. James is a generous, humble, and compassionate man. He felt angry at God and had many questions. It took him two or three hours sitting out in the parking lot, grieving, before he had the courage to come in to visit. I could tell he was so upset. He embraced me with tears of grief and a heart full of love. We sat and talked for about two hours. We prayed, and I found that I was ministering to him, but he was a bigger help to me than I was to him. I praise God for men like James, who are real and show it. Moreover, God loves them even more. I love the way God places people in our lives to help us at all intersections of our journey. James continues to check on me and ask how I am doing. He always has time to hear what I have to say and never seems to be in a rush. He is a true brother in Christ, and I am blessed to have him as a friend.

Again, I go back to the scripture for help in times of sorrow and grief. There are countless scriptures that I could include in this book, but I am only sharing those that have really helped me to go forward. I love Psalm 61:1–3, which states, "Hear my cry, O God; Attend to my prayer. From the end of the earth I will cry to You, When my heart is overwhelmed; Lead me to the rock that is higher than I. For You have been a shelter for me, A strong tower from the enemy."

This is true for me. Many times, I have been overwhelmed

at life, and there are those things that I must continue to do alone. But I am not alone; Jesus my Savior is with me. I have his protection and guidance each hour of the day. He loves me and continues to keep me in his plans and helps me to continue to grow in him. I praise him now and forever more.

Chapter 4

Our Lonely Walk

When Wanda and I traveled, we liked to get off the beaten path and walk. Walking was a chance to see the scenery and stretch our legs. The older one gets, the stiffer one gets in a vehicle. If you have gotten to that great age of discovery, you know what I mean. While travelling through the mountains, we would often walk down to a stream and look at the beautiful things God created for us to enjoy. We would go up trails and discover a beautiful waterfall or a deep ravine that offered unusual wildlife. No matter which walk we would take, it would be an exciting adventure. One summer, we went to Linville Falls in North Carolina, and on a double dare, we hiked to the falls. We were tuckered out, but when we arrived, the view was breathtaking and well worth the hike. That has a special place in my memory bank, and it was such a pleasant trip.

Nothing I did could get me ready for the horrible walk I took on November 1, 2015. This walk was not pleasant at all. I was thankful that God and my mother-in-law were with me. Some walks are not good, not good at all, and you know it before you begin.

Well, all the bad news had come to us; it was the worst news that we had ever received, and we were going to do something next that would completely and utterly tear us apart. We were instructed to go to a room where the nursing staff had prepared for us to see Wanda. I did not want to go, but at the same time, I knew I needed to. Wanda was not there; she had entered into our Savior's arms forever. No more pain, suffering, or questioning, and yes, no more dying, period. I had not even dreamed that this would come so soon in my life. No more dreams of retirement, sipping coffee on the front porch of a townhouse in the mountains. I was expecting this to take place at least twenty more years from now. I dreaded it so much. Phyllis and I began to slowly walk down a narrow hallway very reluctantly. I knew what was coming and had many mixed emotions.

Have you ever traveled down the road with expectation and anticipation of something great about to happen? Well, this was not the case for the two of us. This was the hardest thing I had ever done up to this point of my life. I realized that sooner or later, the tables would be turned for me. I now am a recipient of a ministry that my flock could only give to their pastor. They knew that it would be difficult for me, and I felt and sensed their prayers for me and my family. They hung in there for me and continue to minister to me as their minister. I have the best group of Christian people in the world, bar none. They know me, and I tell them that I love them often. God is so great to me, and I praise him always.

It is a difficult task for me to be on the other side of ministry. I usually do the encouraging and share sympathetic words to the grieving family. Now, it was my turn to receive their warm embrace of love and understanding, as if anyone could understand my grief and loss, but I knew that some of our congregation knew exactly what I was feeling.

Each step I took was as if I had cement in my shoes; it was a chore to pick up one foot and put it in front of the other. It was as if numerous chains were around my feet, and I could not rid myself of them. I experienced times that it was hard to breathe, mingled with total emptiness. I had walked down this hallway with other people as minister, and I still dislike the long, lonely walk. One day, no one will experience this sad walk. I would have done anything rather than walk down to this cold, horrible room. I had not envisioned this part of my life until many more years from now, but I have no control over life and the situations that it brings. All I know, through what I have been promised, is that my God will never leave or forsake me (Hebrews 13:5), and I am so thankful to him for that.

With each step I took, I felt as if I were choking. Not as one having indigestion, but choking as if I had an obstruction in my throat. The closer I got to the doorway, the more I felt as if the walls were going to fall in. This was a real feeling, and I did not like it at all. I wanted to escape this feeling, but I knew that it went along with what I was about to do. This feeling of choking was the reality of the end of life for the one I had loved for over thirty years. Would this feeling ever go away? I asked myself, "Will I ever be able to swallow freely again without this awful sensation in my throat?" I prayed that God would calm my nerves so that I could go through that doorway and into that room. This feeling made these steps even more horrible to take. Although these actions were taking place within my being, I followed through only with God's grace, strength, and direction. I hope I never have this feeling ever again. All I could think of was, what is next? What would be the next horrible feeling that I would have? They came too often, and I could not handle them if it were not for my Lord and Master Jesus, who comforts me. I have the most precious friend and Savior in Jesus.

Phyllis and I took these steps ever so slowly, and now we were at the door. We held hands tighter than ever before. I knew that this would be especially hard for her. Even though she is a strong woman and loved Wanda so much, it all seemed so unreal. I continued to feel that this was a dark, harrowing nightmare that I could not wake up from, the kind of feeling that leaves you all alone, even though others are milling around you.

We allowed the nurse to open the door and we went into that room. There, under the whitest sheet that I have ever seen, was my precious Wanda. My heart filled once again with excruciating sorrow, pain, and loneliness. I began to get weak in the knees and sat down. I only looked for a few minutes and began to weep within my being. I did not realize that I could weep this much, but I found myself in a state of uncontrollable pain. I knew that we all would die one day, but not this soon. I immediately realized that we are not promised tomorrow, but we know who holds tomorrow, and both Wanda and I knew that it was God. I brushed her hair away from her forehead and hoped that she would smile and open her eyes at me. But that was not to be.

All I could envision was her beautiful smile when I looked at her. I knew that she was gone to her reward that God had awaiting her. Both Phyllis and I knew where Wanda was; she was having a great time with all our loved ones, who were welcoming her to heaven. It still hurt down deep in the pit of our stomachs. Not of indigestion, but of heartache. Heartache and indescribable heartbreak was the feeling for the days ahead.

We both sat for about an hour, not really saying anything to each other. Millions of memories flooded my heart and mind as I sat in that room. It was as if the Hoover Dam had broken, and everything flashed through my mind. I knew that Phyllis would have the same feelings, and it was even more difficult for her, since she had given birth to Wanda.

All I could think of were the last words Wanda told me: "Bill, take care of yourself." Today, when people say that to me, I tear up and think of my precious wife. They do not know how hurtful those words are, but I must get through each of them, and God amazingly gives me the strength to sustain me.

Even though we both walked down this hallway into this holding room, we were two people with two very different sets of thoughts and feelings going on within us, two people hurting in similar but very different ways. Thoughts of a daughter taken away much too early, and a husband who longed to spend his final years on mission trips with the love of his life, would be almost too hard to bear. Yet, in our hurt, pain, and despair, while being ripped apart, God continued to love us and give us strength. This strength helped us to get through the day, even though it was difficult, at best. Somehow, only through the grace of our loving God were we able to come to the point of depending upon him for peace. I, now more than ever, value one of the old gospel songs, "One Day at a Time." I am truly taking one day at a time with Jesus within me and beside me, leading me through each aspect in life.

Peace is a real gift from God. Jesus bestowed the Holy Spirit upon the disciples at Pentecost, and we also have that same peace. God immediately filled us with the peace that he offers, and we had no doubts as to where Wanda was. She had only begun to live. Phyllis and I shared a few sentences back and forth with each other; we were in our own way comforting each other by respecting one another with the element of time in this room. We neither pushed the other nor rushed the other to get out of that room. It was our time, and we could stay as long as we wanted. Peace was and is truly a blessing from Almighty God.

One of us finally said, "Are you ready?" We gently stood up, took one more look at Wanda, and exited the room; we started down the hallway, back to where the other people were in the waiting room. With tears in both of our eyes, we grasped each other's hands and held on tighter than before. We walked in disbelief; the other people helped us get back to the vehicle and head back to the parsonage.

My precious church family and friends, who stuck by me, saw the love of God that carried Phyllis and me through these dreadful hours. I hate to even think of going through all these events and not having the grace and peace of God within each of us. It is astounding how God fills us with his love and presence through the Holy Spirit. I continued to embrace my mother-in-law until we got to our vehicle. I praise God for my church family and friends who came to my aid. I shall never forget them as long as I live here on earth, and I will spend eternity with them in heaven. The memory of those special people waiting with me in the hospital, loving me, and praying with me will always remain close to my heart and soul.

Today, whenever I walk down a hallway, I get a bone-chilling feeling within my spirit. I am so cautious about those hallways within a hospital. Perhaps you have been down one of those hallways and know exactly how I feel. In time, God helps us all cope with those aspects of our lives.

I did not adapt well to going home and walking down the hallway to the bedroom. I knew that I would walk down that hallway, but it would be different, very different. Wanda would often pop out of a closet in the hallway and surprise me, and I would stand there, frozen in time, before I said something that made her laugh uncontrollably. I would truly miss her presence when I walked down the hallway to our bedroom. I am glad I have that memory and can recall that special feeling she gave me. Many other things have flooded my mind, and I know in time that I will be able to sort them all out and deal with them in my own way.

These struggles leave a large hole in one's life, but we must take them as they come and adapt. God has a great way of helping us deal with different situations in life that are so unexpected. All of this was unexpected, unplanned, and it continues to be like a bad nightmare that I cannot seem to get over. Many people said to me, "In time, Bill, in time." I do pray that in time I will be able to function in some sort of normal way in life, if there is a normal anymore.

I was blessed to have Phyllis go through this with me. Although it was difficult for both of us, we had each other to lean upon; moreover, we had Jesus to lean on, and he never lets us fall. It was difficult enough to deal with all of this, but it would have been more difficult if Phyllis had been home, and I had to go to Virginia and tell her about Wanda. God orchestrated this for Phyllis to be with me, and we helped each other, along with the remaining family.

It is kind of funny when I think of falling that I may not be able to get up. Wanda would always say, "Don't fall, and you won't have the struggle of getting up." Those little things are not gone forever; they continue to reside in my memory.

The circle of friends that Wanda had has now been broken. Point of Grace sings a song called Circle of Friends, which was sung at the funeral. I can hardly hear it now without getting all emotional; I cry for several hours. The lyrics say that one day, we will be in heaven, and this circle will be restored to its original beauty. Wanda made many friends throughout her short life, and they also became my friends. The Averette University group is still on my mind, and I often wonder how they are doing. Veronica Mau was one of Wanda's dearest friends from way back, and she came down for a visit in 2014.

They were like two young school children, talking and giggling about life. I believe that was one of the best times she had with a friend in some time. The two of them stayed up and talked until three in the morning. Many years had passed and they had time to catch up on all of life's situations.

Angela Eckler was a great lifelong friend of Wanda's. Wanda was with Angela when she birthed her first daughter, Kathryn, and her second daughter, Grace. I remember the times that they were talking about the babies coming and all the wonderful things that Wanda was going to do for them. We all had good times together, and Wanda especially loved Angela's farm life. Wanda even loved the description her girls gave of a chicken dish that she made; they called it "disgusting chicken," and I still have the recipe. We often ate supper together, and some type of animal would make Wanda have those "bluckky" feelings of almost wanting to spew her food all over the area. The girls loved the fact that Auntie Wanda's favorite color was vibrant neon green. Angela and Wanda were like sisters, and they swapped a Christmas ball each year with a gift inside it. I have that silver ball, but I could not put a gift in it this year. That was a special memory for the two of them. One day, Angela, we will be reunited with our special friends and family, and Wanda will be right there with them. Our circle of friends will be back together.

Today, when I hear this song, Circle of Friends, by Point of Grace, I can smile a little, for I know that those friends and loved ones are having a fabulous time with Wanda. At times, I wish that I was already with them, but I know that my time will come soon enough. This life we live continues to be a fleeting vapor and gets even shorter as we get older. When we were children, we thought it would take forever for Christmas to come around again. We had no cares and worries of the world, like we do now. It seems like each year gets faster and faster. When we get to heaven, time will not be like we see it: "But, beloved, do not forget this one thing, that with the Lord one day is as a thousand years, and a thousand years as one day" (2 Peter 3:8). This really excites me to no end. Are you ready? I sure am.

Chapter 5

I Only Said, "See You Later"

When I entered the house that we called our home, it was not the same. Everywhere I looked, I saw Wanda's fingerprints; they were on everything we had in the house. It hurt deep down inside, and I did not know if I could bear this pain, but suddenly, God gave me an amazing peace. It was all right. No matter how strong I was supposed to be as a man, I could not hold back the tears of grief. The more I thought of our life together, the more I cried. Talking helped at times, but it really was terrible when everyone left me and I was alone. The house was empty and full of void for me, and I did not know how to fix it. I realized that I could not fix all of this. Many things in life are not fixable, but I knew that Jesus Christ could fix it. Sleep and rest seemed to be nothing I wanted or needed at this time. I did not want to eat anything. I forced myself to eat what little I did. The more talking I did seemed to help a little. My life was a wreck. I was torn apart, and only God could put me back together again. I had to depend upon him for everything. I was reminded that I am the clay in my father's hands. He would remake me.

Many hours passed, and the feeling of numbness was more

real than ever. More family members arrived, and our church people cooked enough food for an army. I continued to find myself in disbelief and pinched my arm to see if all of this was real. It was, but as Wanda would say, I had to "put my best foot forward." I did not want to, but I knew that I must try to continue living. The house was so full but so very empty. I saw Wanda's fingerprints on literally everything I looked toward.

My good friend Billy Mahn came and took me for a ride around the community to get out of the house for a while. I cried as he comforted me, and getting out of the house helped in a big way. Billy is a gentle giant, and I appreciated that. He has a heart as soft as a marshmallow but does not want anyone to know it. That day he took me out around the community did more for me than he will ever know. I had an opportunity to vent a little and come to grips with all that had happened. I was thankful to my good friend for driving me around. I will never forget his abundant love that was expressed to me in such a short amount of time. He continues to be a great friend and seems like a father to me at times. We can have fun and be serious about God and his love for us.

After arriving back at the parsonage, I found the house full of more people, with more food. Finally, the remaining family members arrived, and we experienced another outpouring of tears and grief. This was such a shock and everything happened quickly. It was very difficult to process through. Rev. Tommy Gaskin, my good friend and pastor, was by my side, comforting me and helping me get through all of this. I sure was thankful to have some pastor friends to call upon in my time of grief. Come to think of it, I did not call them; they automatically arrived when I needed them. God does things like that, you know. He instantly takes care of the needs we have. It's hard to explain the exhaustion we all have. If you've been through the death of a loved one, then you know what I mean.

The next day, we went to Belk Funeral Home to pick out everything we needed for the celebration of life service. Sidney Belk could not believe all of this and was as shocked as we were. After spending about three hours picking out flowers and the rest, we were spent and drove back home. All of the arrangements were made; I only had to ask Tommy and my nephew, Rev. Sidney Calhoun, to conduct the funeral service. This was perhaps one of the most difficult things I have had to do. But it had to be done. I always thought I would be the one to go to heaven first. But we do not have a choice; the only thing we must do is to be ready for God to call out our names.

When all the people left for the evening, J. R., Wanda's brother, and I stayed up talking until about three in the morning. We could not stop talking about this wonderful sister and wife. She was a remarkable woman. She loved her family and the simple things in life. She often told me that the best things in life were not money to go see a movie or eat a meal, but time together to sit and talk. She had wisdom beyond her years. Almost every Friday night, Wanda and I went out for a night on the town at a special restaurant. We called this our date night. What a wonderful time those nights were, even if we had other couples with us. Our people saw that we were real and did not put on airs.

Life is not the same. I will miss those wonderful Friday night dates, but I long to see her when it will never be night again, in heaven, where the Son is always shining.

The night of the visitation at the funeral home was exhausting for all of us. I never heard the words, "I am sorry," so many times before. People I have never seen before came and paid their respects. People traveled from many places encouraging me with support and love. It seemed like the night would never end. I was overwhelmed by all the people who came to the visitation and came by the house. We were having God's love and strength poured out upon us. I longed for people to embrace me and not say anything. Others who had experienced the same loss understood and could sympathize more easily. I still could not believe I was standing in a funeral home. It should have been me. Wanda was way too young. She was only fifty-four years old. But God does not make any mistakes, and he knows the very best. I thank God for what I have, not what I have lost. It took me a few months to realize this fact. Memories, compassion, and the embrace of God have helped me make it thus far in life, but it continues to be very difficult.

I asked Otis Lawhon, our music minister, to take Wanda's CD's and pick five upbeat, happy Christian songs for the funeral on Wednesday. He took the CD's and he chose five of the most special songs that Wanda loved. I knew that this would be a difficult task for Otis. Wanda was one of the high sopranos in the choir and could get to the highest notes in the Christmas and Easter musicals that we would sing each year. I miss seeing her, and her place in the choir is so lonely looking. Wanda wanted her funeral to be a happy occasion and wanted us to praise Jesus for salvation.

I listened to all the things that Tommy and Sidney said about Wanda, and all of them were true. Oh, how she loved life, children, her family, and her Savior Jesus. I sat between the two women who were left in my life, who made such an impact upon me. Sitting between my mother and mother-in-law was such a comfort. You see, it had been about twenty years for both of them since they had lost their husbands, and they knew what I was going through. At one point, I found my hands shaking because of the pain and grief I was experiencing. And at the next moment, I unexpectedly raised my hand in praise to God for all he does. All I knew is that my hands flew up, and I felt the peace of Jesus. I am not ashamed of my Savior and Lord.

I looked around me and saw all my pastor friends and was overwhelmed to think they thought that much of Wanda and me. They were there for me, and I was thankful to all of them. I looked at the children, and every one of them had tears in their eyes. Most of the women were shedding tears over the loss of such a wonderful Christian woman, who was a friend and buddy. The deacons who were pallbearers were crying. You see, Wanda had a great impact on all people. She loved Jesus, and therefore she loved everyone. One day, she went to embrace a woman in the sanctuary, but she rudely jerked away. I told her not to worry about it, and she immediately said that it was their loss. And she was right. That woman never did smile, and to this day, she does not smile. Wanda was so concerned about her and even wondered if she was a Christian. I knew that others saw what happened, but we all loved that woman anyway. I pray for that woman and hope she can get over her bitterness and anger. She constantly frowns, and is rude to others in church. Her expression is as if she had been eating lemons all her life. She seems to have very few friends and others can see why that is the case. I continue to pray for her to get the joy of Jesus in her life, if in fact she is a Christian. Only Jesus knows.

After all the songs were sung and the words were said, it was time to exit the church building. It was difficult to get started. The entire church was packed. I sang the last song on the way out and did what Wanda wanted me to do: praise Jesus. I knew that she was already enjoying the benefits of heaven and Jesus. She was only beginning to live. Oh, what a wonderful time she is having.

As we were praising Jesus, I said, "See you later, Wanda." Wanda and I always said that. We never said good-bye. We always said, "See you later." I know that she somehow was saying the same thing to all of us that November day.

We walked out to the vehicles and got ready to proceed to the cemetery for the graveside services. Sidney drove Phyllis and me. It was not a good ride at all. We were quiet and reserved. All that could be said was said, and then our lives had to go on. It seemed like it took forever for all the people to get to the cemetery. Rev. Sidney Calhoun and Rev. Frankie Tanner shared at the cemetery. After the prayers were prayed and a song was sung, it was time to leave. All the pallbearers came by, and then the children came over. Wanda loved all of them so much.

One of the children said to me, "Pastor Bill, you're not going to leave us too, are you?"

I said, "No, son, I am not. I will be here for a while longer."

You talk about tearing out someone's heart. This tore me up even more. There was a young man named Trevor at the cemetery, who said he did not believe in God. I was led to go over to him and share Jesus with him. The seeds were planted, and I only pray that they take root and grow in this young man's heart and soul.

Hopefully, something I said, our something someone said may have penetrated this young man's way of thinking. I believe that he will remember those words that were said that day. I only hope and pray that he accepts Jesus as Savior before it is too late for him.

After visiting at the cemetery, we went back to the house and changed clothes and relaxed for a while. More people came by with more of the "sacred fowl" (chicken) and other food. I was truly blessed by all the love and compassion poured out on me and my family. I believe it also overwhelmed some of my family members.

After I changed clothes, I just sat on my sofa, but everything I saw reminded me of Wanda. All of the dishes, her desk in the den, her pocketbook, her closet, and countless other things reminded me of her. I even caught a drift of her scent; the kind of perfume she wore. Could I go on? Would I go on? Yes, I must go on and do the best I can and spread the love of Jesus with others in the community and world. That is what Jesus is all about.

Going on would be difficult at best, but I must go forward, as bad as it hurts down inside my soul. I knew that each day would bring on different decisions to make, and I always prayed for Christ to lead me in those decisions. Things like paying the bills, washing laundry, ironing, and cleaning all would bring back pain in these mundane activities. Many times, I thought I was the only one going through the death of a spouse, but I realized that there are millions of people who find themselves living alone now. It is not the best option, but it is better than the alternative. Maybe it is not. It would be better to be with Jesus than to be here alone, but for now, I must remain here, alone. To be honest, I am not alone at all. Jesus is within me. God continues to take care of me, and I feel the power of the Holy Spirit even more in my life.

Life continues on, and I see Wanda every day that I live. I truly miss how she would be aggravated at me when I would get up early in the morning and begin singing in the shower. She would clear her throat and tell me to be quiet or go somewhere. I thought it was funny, and I really miss that, especially on Saturday mornings. She was a night owl and wanted to sleep until the last minute before getting ready for the day. She always said that she slept better the last two hours than all night long. Now I see what she meant.

Sleepless nights came and went. Some nights, I feel like she is right beside me, and I feel her presence. It was very difficult on our anniversary; December 13 was our special day. I could not get anything accomplished. I had to finish a project we were working on for our family and friends for a Christmas gift, *Seasons 2016,* a weekly devotion book, but it was not half finished. I had to scurry around and finish, like yesterday. Somehow, I was able to get all the work finished, through laughter and tears, and I was happy with it. I knew that Wanda would have been happy also, despite a few errors along the way. No matter how many people you get to read a document for spelling, spacing, and punctuation, there are always mistakes. After rereading the document, I took it to get printed and was happy to have it wrapped for this year's Christmas present.

On the night of our anniversary, I felt so alone. I thought of the almost thirty years that we had together, and it was all too short. I tried to be happy, but nothing I did got me in that mood, so I stopped trying to do that. At around one thirty in the morning, I began to pray to my rock, Jesus Christ. I told him that I was so desperately lonely. I asked Jesus to please tell Wanda happy anniversary and say that I loved her so much. I had immediate assurance that Jesus would do that for me. I had a tremendous feeling of love and joy; I never felt that before. It was as if the window flew open and I caught a breath of fresh air that filled me up to my toes. I was so overwhelmed that all I could do was cry. This time, they were tears of joy, for I knew that Jesus did what I asked him to do. I have no doubts that he answered my urgent prayer. I heard Jesus say, "It is done, Bill." What a blessing and comfort.

Many times, I have felt the Lord embracing me, and his eternal comfort helped me get through the night and into the next day. I cannot tell you how wonderful my God has been to me through the loss of Wanda. Comfort from God has helped me look at myself in a different light. I value more the time with my Father in prayer, and each day, I pray more times than I can count on my hands. Sometimes, the concise short pointed prayers make the most difference in life especially when you are alone again and begin a new life.

I do miss my prayer and Bible reading partner so much, but I have never lost my Savior Jesus Christ. I thank God for his everlasting love and forgiveness of sins, and I know that I will be joining Wanda and others who have gone on to heaven before me. Prayer is as essential to the Christian as a sail and anchor is to a ship.

I cannot tell you the many times people at Black Creek Church have dropped by my office to see how I was doing. At times, I'd get teary-eyed, and we'd pray. Other times, I'd find myself laughing but end up weeping. The people who dropped by understood, and we'd wind up praising Jesus for Wanda's life and for heaven that is awaiting us. Some people did not know what to say, but just a smile, handshake, or nod helped me so much. These people are true brothers and sisters in Christ, and when we leave one another's company, I only say, "I'll see you later."

Wanda and I never liked the words "good-bye." We thought they were so final. We thought that they were cold and bitter words. That we would never see someone again was not a thought that would enter our minds or our hearts. Each day, we would kiss each other and say, "See you later." We always did that, and at the funeral, I told Wanda that again. I will see her later. I will see her later in her new body and new clothes, and she will be smiling like a mule eating briers. You know, one of those wide beautiful smiles that we see on our loved one's face after being surprised by a party. Many friends have come and gone our way, and we always told them, "See you later," instead of good-bye.

If people were hiding in the house, they would think that I am crazy, because I still tell Wanda that I will see her later. When I come in to eat, I constantly look for her. Again, after reality strikes again and again, I realize that she is not here. I have my time and get on with the chores that I have to do. Somehow, God keeps me going, and that gives me a reason to continue on in life. Wanda would not want me to pine away for her but to celebrate life to the fullest.

I remember that Wanda loved to take the Children in Action to eat at Cici's Pizza. Recently, I took five of the boys there to eat pizza. I really enjoyed it, and so did they. The reason they were taken out to eat was because they all answered a biblical question. This was there big reward. Little things like that really mean a great deal to these young boys, and I got a great deal of joy doing that for them. We celebrated as we ate, and one of the boys reminded me that this was one of Mrs. Wanda's favorite places to eat. Well, I don't know about that, but she did enjoy it a lot, as did the others who traveled with her. To Wanda, I only said, "See you later." I will see her again, real soon. In heaven we will never be separated and will not experience any heartache, pain, and will enjoy peace and rest eternally. That is wonderful to think about.

Chapter 6

So Full, Yet So Empty

The other day, someone asked me how I was doing, and I responded with this simple phrase: "Tremendous emptiness and incredible fullness." I could have asked, "How can one be so full, yet so empty?" Seems illogical, but it is quite realistic for me.

Not long after the shock and utter void, I sat down with the Welsh Neck Baptist Association's director of missions, Rev. Dave Worthington, and we talked. One of the first things I said was, "How can one be so full, yet so empty?" He said that that was a good question, and we discussed it further. Pastor Dave has been a great help to me during this unexpected horrible experience of losing a spouse. He has always made time for me and has always encouraged me to continue in life. I told Pastor Dave that I was going to write a book that I hoped will help other Christian servants as they journey through their loss. That was eight months ago, and I am continuing to write and rewrite many things.

I expressed to Pastor Dave that I feel full from the love of God but also empty and alone. We talked about God's precious love and how he fills us in times of great turmoil and need.

After a rather lengthy session, I felt relieved and somewhat better, but I continued to feel empty. How was I going to handle this? Would I ever get over this emptiness? I knew that I needed to trust God even more in my life and depend on him more. After all, God and my Savior, through the power of the Holy Spirit, is all I really have. When I have that, I need no one but king Jesus.

All my joy had been taken from me. I was not as joyous as I once was, and I felt empty at the same time. I hated feeling like this. It is almost like the optimist versus the pessimist. Is the glass half-full or half-empty? Well, I had feelings of both at the same time, and I knew that was not at all normal (if there is anything called normal). I felt full in the fact that God loved me and poured his compassion upon me, but at the same time, I had feelings of being empty and dry. These dry and empty feelings came from not having my precious Wanda with me. The more I did in life, the emptier and fuller I became. Yes, I know it seems odd, but that is the feelings I had and continue to have.

I thought about trying a grief support group but decided not to go, until a friend of mine invited me to go after he lost his wife. Lon G. Howle and I sat on the back of my truck for three hours and exchanged feelings over losing our wives. His wife passed about a week after I lost Wanda. He told me about a grief support group; I went one time, and it seemed to help. Later, I accidentally ran into our associational counselor, Dr. Lisa Willard, at the mission's office, and we sat down and talked. I visited her for about three months, and those sessions helped me a great deal, but I continued to feel full and empty at the same time. It seemed like a Catch-22 situation.

How can this be? I asked myself. I feel full of the love, leadership, and joy of Christ in my life, and at the same time, I feel lost in a lonesome room, with no one to talk to. Mind you, I have been speaking and praying to Jesus for many years and still do so. I communicate with God concerning his overwhelming love, guidance, and presence in my life. I cannot make it each day without my wonderful God leading me. Almost everything I see now, I value even more in life. God has been so wonderful to me, and I am finding there are many ways to tell people that. Most of the time, I find many opportunities to share my Savior's love. I love that, and I love telling people about Jesus and what God has done (and is doing) for me.

I love the Bible, for it is God's holy word, and I receive many important truths to live by each day. The other day, I visited a pastor friend in the hospital and read Psalm 142 to him. I went back and reread verses 1 through 3. These words have been giving me great comfort in my days of loneliness and struggles as I view my own situation. These precious words have helped me so much. I love it when God reveals his presence and love toward me: "I cry out to the LORD with my voice; with my voice to the LORD I make my supplication. I pour out my complaint before Him; I declare before Him my trouble. When my spirit was overwhelmed within me, Then You knew my path." The emphasis is, "Then You knew my path." God has been leading me down a new path that has been more fulfilling as a Christian and as a single person. It is a difficult thing, trying to live alone again. This one thing I know: God is always leading me, and I always feel his presence.

Another scripture that has comforted me is Philippians 4:13. I like to call this my life verse, and I seek strength in it each day that I live: "I can do all things through Christ who strengthens me." I truly can, and you can too. It is simply a matter of faith and total surrender to our Lord for all he does in our lives. Today, many people have a shallow faith, but if it is shallow, it needs to be pointed at, keyed into, and focused upon the Cross of Christ. Without the Cross of Christ, we are nothing. Jesus is my all-in-all, and I cannot take one step unless he empowers me to go forward.

There are many scriptures I have found to be a great comfort to me, and I read them almost daily. They have become a part of who I am; I have memorized some of them. God is good to us all the time, and all the time, God is good to us. I find so much assurance in the scriptures, and I have really seen these words come to life more for me than ever before. If words are not thought about, believed in, and digested, they can never become a part of one's theology. I believe that every word Jesus said is true and that there are no errors or contradictions in them. Here are some words from Jesus that are more special to me than they have ever been in my life; they give me total assurance:

> Let not your heart be troubled; you believe in God, believe also in Me. In My Father's house are many mansions, if *it were* not *so*, I would have told you. I go to prepare a place for you. And if I go and prepare a place for you, I will come again and receive you to Myself; that where I am, *there* you may be also. And where I go you know, and the way you know." Thomas said to Him, "Lord, we do not know where You are going, and how can we know the way?" Jesus said to him, "I am the way, the truth, and the life. No one comes to the Father except through Me" (John 14:1–6).

These instructions from Jesus are true and life-changing. There is nothing in this world that I should be troubled about. When I have Jesus and believe in God my Father, I have nothing to worry about. As Wanda would say, nothing good can come from "worryation." This word is a combination of "worry" and "aggravation." God has always taken care of me, and he always will. I have that absolute truth and assurance, and I will live with him eternally.

The other day, sitting at the table for supper, I got so emotional. All of a sudden, these words came to me: "I will never leave you nor forsake you" (Hebrews 13:5b). God at his own special time comes to us and fills us with his love and warmth, so we can continue in life. If we are in Christ, then he comes in our soul, and he never leaves us. It may be that we decide to leave him, but he never leaves us. "Never" means "not a chance." That is absolute and can be taken to the bank. Again, I had those feelings of being full, and yet so empty. Losing a loving wife in life stinks a great deal. It really stinks, and I do not like it, but it is what it is. Wanda made a big impact on my life, and she left a huge hole that only God can fill. She was ready to go be with Jesus, and I was left behind to do more work in the vineyard for our Savior. I must keep on keeping on. I get all of that, but I still have many struggles. Struggles always seem to be a part of life. One day all of those struggles will be over for those who believe and trust in Jesus Christ for salvation.

Time goes on in life, and things change forever. I traveled to the North Carolina mountains in Rutherfordton for my family Christmas gathering. For the first time in twenty-nine years, Wanda was not by my side. I went through the door and fell apart, and my mother was there to help me pick up the pieces. She understood all of my feelings, and after a short time, we were laughing at some of the things Wanda would say at this very special time of the year. If Wanda had her way about life, every day would have been Christmas. I believe in some ways it is, because we are supposed to celebrate Christ each day of our lives.

All the family members came in for supper, and by the grace of God, we were able to get through the family Christmas pretty well. All of the children had a blast.

Later in the month, I traveled to Virginia to have Christmas with the Powell's. As usual, the table was filled with all kinds of Christmas treats to eat, and we had our usual prime rib for Christmas supper. We were all feeling down, and all of a sudden, Rob, my nephew, asked his wife, Alyssa, if she wanted a soda to drink.

She immediately said, "You know I can't have them now."

That made me suspect that she may be pregnant. Sure enough, Rob announced that he had a picture of the ultrasound to show us. We were all laughing and happy to hear the news. Somehow, I felt down deep inside of me that Bobby, Wanda's late father both knew even before we did. Happy moments help us drag through the struggles of life. Before long we will have a bouncing baby boy in the family named Elijah Joseph Powell.

On my way back to Darlington, I was reflecting on the family gatherings at both places, and I realized how blessed I am. I turned on those special songs that Wanda loved; they all seemed to be on the same CD that I put into the player. I prayed, sung, cried, laughed, and prayed some more. At one point, I had to pull off of the road and sit awhile. I found myself praising God in my grief. I thought, *Will I ever get back to a normal life? There may not be a normal life anymore. As long as I have King Jesus, I am all right. No one can take me away from him, no matter how hard they try. If anything, I am more dedicated to him than ever.*

Guess what came up next? Tax time; yes, tax time. I had no idea. Wanda was my accountant, so I had to muddle through our receipts and documents, and try to fill those forms out as best as I could. I spoke to Wanda often. I spent three or four weeks separating and analyzing papers. At one point, I believe Wanda kept the chewing gum wrappers to account for the money she spent. I found Bo Jangle's, McDonald's, Burger King, and Hardees receipts all crammed in an envelope. I said, "Wanda, what have you done here?" She would have gotten a kick out of me finding all those food receipts. As I sifted, separated, and scrambled through papers, I finally got to the bottom of all the year's receipts. I had not looked in the notebook where Wanda had finalized everything. After all this, I took the book and turned to the last page, and there it was. I did not need to go through all those papers at all. Wanda had put all the things I needed on a piece of paper and wrote, "Bill, here are the documents for this year's taxes." I screamed so loud that it startled my dog, Chip.

Somehow, I believe that Wanda had known something I was not aware of. If she did, I truly wished she would have told me. She never gave an inclination, one way or another. I will never know, but on second thought, I may not need to know, and it may not have made a difference. I was able to get the taxes finished and all the estimates paid on time. I believe that she would have been proud of the fact that I struggled and made it. I miss her so much, and I long to see her again.

Taxes were now finished, and another difficult time of the year came. Valentine's Day was so special to us. It was not only a day for people in love, it was also my birthday. Boy, you talk about a double whammy. Yes, a double dog-stinking whammy. I had not gone through any depression until now. For about three or four weeks, I was so depressed that I did not want to do anything. All I wanted to do was to sleep; hoping that somehow all the pain and suffering would go away. I replayed that horrific ride behind the ambulance in my mind. I thought of all the people who ministered to me. I felt the cold chill of that walkway, and the chilling room where Wanda was lying. I replayed every awful aspect of life that leads to eternal life. How could I be so depressed? I had to get out of this situation. I had to do it in a hurry, or I would not survive.

I immediately reflected on my salvation experience and recalled how Wanda and I met. We both had the abundant love of Jesus in our hearts and souls. Nothing could separate us from the love that Jesus gave us. I realized that I continued to possess that love; Jesus cared for me more than I ever thought. I did not go to a psychiatrist (or any other doctor, for that matter). Other people I spoke to were friends and ministry colleagues. I loved God, and I knew that he would get me out of this situation. God once again carried me through, and I am blessed by the awesome spirit of peace, guidance, and assurance that he gives me. Assurance that he was with me all the time empowered me to overcome this depression. I believe that Satan threw this depression at me to destroy me. But the joke is on Satan; it did not destroy me at all. If anything, it made me a stronger person and more dedicated to Christ.

Once again, the scriptures came to my mind and heart. I recalled this wonderful truth that Christ has given us, that helps us in many ways:

> For I am persuaded that neither death nor life, nor angels nor principalities nor powers, nor things present nor things to come, nor height nor depth, nor any other created thing, shall be able to separate us from the love of God which is in Christ Jesus our Lord (Romans 8:38–39).

That is real hope and assurance for the believer in Christ Jesus. This is true and is evident in the lives of many people. God continued to love me, no matter how many feelings I had. He continues to love me and keeps me in the palm of his hand. I feel him in everything I do and am so thankful to my God and creator for all he does, especially salvation in Jesus Christ.

Also, in my weakness, I found the great strength of God in 2 Corinthians 12:9, where Paul says, "And He said to me, 'My grace is sufficient for you, for my strength is made perfect in weakness.' Therefore most gladly I will rather boast in my infirmities, that the power of Christ may rest upon me." In my frailties and mortal being, I become weak at times. It is God who in our weakness in life makes us strong. This strength is astronomical and is unexplainable at times, but it is there when we so desperately need it. If you notice, the scripture said that the strength of Christ would be made perfect in our weakness. The strength that Christ gives us is a force that helps us get up and go forward in life. Without Christ, I am nothing. Without Christ in our individual lives, we are all nothing.

Our strength is renewed like an eagle. Last year on vacation, I was able to see a rare sight on a lake in Virginia. I saw two bald eagles; they were simply beautiful. One of the graceful birds was soaring higher and higher, and all of a sudden, it dove into the water and came up with a large fish in its claws. God tells us that in our weakness, we will have our strength renewed like an eagle. We find this in Isaiah 40:31: "But those who wait on the LORD Shall renew *their* strength; They shall mount up with wings like eagles, They shall run and not be weary, They shall walk and not faint." Notice that this said that this occurs to those who wait upon the Lord. We will be able to do more in life and not get exhausted. Our Lord does give us rest when we wait upon him in the right frame of mind.

When I feel my strength and direction failing me, I can always go back to the scripture and find that amazing strength and grace that only our Lord gives us. And what an amazing grace that is! Free for those who desire to have that grace, and it is readily available. All we have to do is ask our wonderful Savior to be merciful to us, and he immediately forgives us of our sins.

I find that I have become a more humble person throughout my loss and growing closer to our heavenly Father. God cares for us more than we can even fathom in our finite minds. I am constantly seeking inspiring words from the Bible to help me in my Christian pilgrimage. And you know what? God always comes through for me. One such place is found in 1 Peter 5:6–10.

> Therefore humble yourselves under the mighty hand of God, that He may exalt you in due time, casting all your care upon Him, for He cares for you. Be sober, be vigilant; because your adversary the devil walks about like a roaring lion, seeking whom he may devour. Resist him, steadfast in the faith, knowing that the same sufferings are experienced by your brotherhood in the world. But may the God of all grace, who called us to His eternal glory by Christ Jesus, after you have suffered a while, perfect, establish, strengthen, and settle you.

The more I humble myself under the mighty hand of God, according to this scripture, the more I realize that I cannot make it through my Christian journey without Christ. Even at my lowest time, when I lost my wife, God exalted me due to his great love for me. Satan wanted nothing more than to destroy me after the loss I faced, but God gives me the strength each day to conquer and even excel at being his servant. Suffering does come as a Christian, but God gives us a sense of being settled, because of his awesome love and care. This gives me great courage, comfort, and a greater desire to serve God and become a better minister to the people I love and serve each week.

Feeling full and empty at the same times seems so contradictory. If you have been where I am, then you know what I am thinking of, and what I am experiencing in life right now. This tremendous emptiness is that life seems to lead to a dead end, or at least for some time felt that way. It could be described as scraping the bottom of the barrel and getting nothing from within. Cold, damp, musty, alone, and unappealing could best describe the emptiness I experienced. No one wants to experience this every day of their lives. It could drive you to a point of no return. Thank God that it never drove me to that point, and I believe I did not go to that point because of God's great love and care for me. This could also be expressed in solitude. Solitude is perhaps a good place to visit, but I sure do not want to live in that state the remainder of my life.

On the other hand, this incredible fullness is that part of life which becomes astoundingly joyful, happy, fulfilled, and assured, to use only a few words. This has only been experienced by the love of Almighty God, through my Savior Jesus Christ. It was imperative that I make the conscious choice to either wallow in self-pity and remain in the emptiness, or see the blessings that God has given me (and those he has in store for me). I made the right decision: to go with the latter, rather than the former, and see the wonderful life God continues to have for me to enjoy. A great part of that is found in the church family, friends, and family members I have grown to love and cherish so much. They all have helped me recognize that even though there's a void in my life, I can continue to enjoy great fullness in our Lord and Savior Jesus Christ. I had always known that, but I needed to be told that several times before it actually permeated into my being. I am thankful for those people who have brought me to a new awakening to life and the joy it automatically brings.

In April of each year, we would travel to Land's End at Myrtle Beach to take a short get away from the busyness of life. By this time, we would be somewhat tired and need to rest from all those people "chewing" on us from time to time. You know, every now and then, everyone wants to get away from it all, for a couple of days. Only this year, I could not find the strength to go to the beach. I could not bring myself to go to where so many memories had been built, even though they were wonderful. This was one place that Wanda truly loved to vacate, as she dropped her gears in neutral. I did not mind doing that either; quite frankly, I enjoyed it, but not this close to all that happened.

In June, I traveled to Buggs Island Lake in Virginia, where the Powell family was vacationing. It was tolerable, and everyone had a pleasant time. The only problem was that everything was so different. I knew it would be, and a few times I got teary, but we all made it through, and we all had a good time. Alyssa and Rob could not come all week. She was so pregnant that the doctor told her to stay around the house, just in case the baby came. Rob was able to come for a night and day, and of course, he caught the largest fish. Rob is so darn lucky. He could catch a fish without a hook on the line. J. R. and Amanda went out, mostly in the early mornings, and caught a few fish. All in all, we had a good time, but by Friday, we were all ready to get back home. Vacation is good, but getting home is better.

July was very, very difficult for me, but even in the emptiness and fullness, I was able to carry on. Usually on July 4, we would get up early, at 5:30; it was Wanda's idea for us to wash windows and do our annual spring-in-the-summer cleaning. We would do it, and by around eleven in the morning, we would go eat breakfast at Shoney's or I-Hop. Afterwards, we would come back home and fall out with exhaustion for the remainder of the day. I did the entire house, except the den; I figured it could wait a little longer.

July 5 was Wanda's birthday. I was in a sad state that day, but God gave me plenty to do to keep me busy, and it was not as difficult as I thought it would be. You see, when you begin to have your own little pity party, God gets your attention. It did not take long at all for me to look around and see that others were worse off than me. Other people have lost a great deal more than I have, but they continued on, and so did I. All in all, God has shown himself to be Almighty and worthy, and he has met my every need. God continues to meet my needs and I am astonished at all he does for me.

In my times of loneliness, awkwardness, spiritual upheaval, rediscovery, and reconstruction, God has not once left me. I am so grateful for his abiding presence, patience, and understanding of all that I have been experiencing. Now, I find myself reading more than I have ever read in my life. Reading helps motivate me to keep on doing what God has called me to do in life. Whether it is for my service as a minister, or for fun, reading seems to help clear my head and redirect my priorities and goals in life.

On July 16, my great-nephew, Elijah Joseph Powell, was born. I have not held him yet, but I know that it will be an emotional time for me. I have seen many pictures, and he is a handsome little boy. He gets his great appearance from both his mother and father. I am sure that other traits will show up later from other relatives. I look forward to telling him about his great-auntie who is living in heaven. Wanda would have been so proud of little E. J., as she was proud of all her family. Somehow, I know in the depths of my soul that she and her daddy knew that little E. J. would be coming to fill our lives with joy and happiness. God always knows what he is doing, and he does it well. Dr. Randall Jones, an evangelist from South Carolina, spoke at a revival at Black Creek Baptist Church once, and he said, "When God shows up, he shows out." I tend to agree with Dr. Jones and have found this to be true. We can never out-pray, out-give, out-serve, out-talk, or out-love God for all he does for us. He is our loving, awesome heavenly Father. One day, those who are saved and have been washed in the blood of Christ will see him and never be taken away from him. Amen and Glory Hallelujah! I am sure that you will agree with me.

My life continues to go onward, with a few ups and downs, as anyone's will, but those are so hard to take when there is only one to experience them. This is one of life's realities, and I get through them as best as I can. God continues to help me, and without him, I would be a large heap of rubble. I thank God that I am not, and I continue moving forward, even though it is difficult at times. I continue to remain empty, but at the same time, I am full of God's blessings in my life. I can never thank him enough for all he has done for me.

Chapter 7

Stuck in the Middle

I was the middle child from a loving family. Both my younger sister and older brother looked to me as kind of a buffer when things were hectic in life. Many times, I felt like I remained stuck in the middle of things that were going on, not in a bad way, but as a challenging opportunity. I like challenges, and I love to be a part of seeing things move forward. However, I continue to feel stuck in the stages of grief. I have not been depressed, so to speak, only readjusting.

What is grief? Grief is a conglomeration of responses from within regarding some special entity that has died, where there is a loss of a relationship that was formed. Grief is a difficult situation to handle. I have been through all the stages of grief, but all of a sudden, I will be blasted again by one of the stages. When I think the day is going to be good, it happens: I fall to pieces and get very emotional. People often say that it will get better, and for the most part it has, but out of the blue, some very small memory will blow me out of the water. Those small memories are very special but hit me at the most inopportune times. I wish that I could control when and what comes my way, but I cannot. I take it as it comes, and tears begin to flow.

I used to be ashamed to cry in front of people, but when I feel my emotions flare up, I cannot help myself. I know that I need to let it out or else those emotions will blow me wide open and cause other problems. Just like the cream in between an Oreo cookie, I feel stuck in the middle at times. When people ask me to go out to eat or on a short day trip, I feel like I am the third wheel. They always assure me that I am not, and they encourage me to go with them. I usually go ahead and have a good time with the people, and it seems to help a great deal. I have found that the more I get out and do things for others, the better I am able to handle my own situations. I suppose that is therapy, in and of itself. These things that I discover that can help me advance in life as a productive citizen do not require a doctor's visit (or a fee).

I know that these are the stages of grief: denial (and isolation), anger, bargaining, depression, and acceptance. Even though I have been through all of these stages of grief and loss, I continue to somewhat feel stuck in the middle. I had taken courses on helping others handle their grief, but it had never attacked me, and I have been processing through all the stages.

Yes, I have been through the denial and isolation, and I continue to deal with it. Denial is an unconscious defense mechanism used to reduce anxiety by denying ones thoughts, feelings, or facts that are consciously intolerable. I do not believe that you completely master those grief stages. It is a work in progress; it seems to jump on you and often shows up, sometimes even harder. I still cannot believe my wife is gone. I see her fingerprints on everything in the house, and her influence is within my entire life. It is difficult to continue at times, but I know that she would want me to keep living. I have no doubts as to where she is: She is in the arms of Jesus in heaven.

The shock will never wear off. When the doctor said that he did all he could but could not save her, I began to weep uncontrollably and felt as though I was choking. I have never felt this way before in my life. I felt as if Satan put his slimy, hot hand down my throat and ripped out my heart. Today, almost a year has passed, and I continue to have some of those feelings. I may never get them all out of my mind and heart. All I know is that God has helped to eliminate the severity of those feelings so that I can face each new day. The shock of hearing that your wife is gone is real and devastating. Denial does play some part in all these difficult emotions. Every evening for about three or four months, I would drive up to the house, see Wanda's Jeep, and look forward to a kiss and a big hug from her. It hit me, and I would be devastated and relive these emotions all over again. The pain of my loss set in, and I did not even want to go out to the mailbox, but I pushed myself, for I knew it was a healthy thing to do.

Isolation is keeping to oneself and withdrawing from society. This is a real problem. At times, I want to isolate myself from others for the simple fact that Wanda and I did everything together. We went to the grocery store, shopped for clothes, ate out, and went to church or to other social events, always together. The easiest way for me to isolate myself is to find a silly excuse to stay at home. Sleeping is the best way to isolate oneself from the world and those friends who care about you. After a few weeks, I was able to master that, but at times, it jumps back on me, and I have to fight to overcome it. And I always win the battle (at least for a period of time).

Although isolation and loneliness are not stages of grief I was overwhelmed with these two aspects and found it more difficult than I had expected. I really expected these feelings to only last a few days. Loneliness is another phase that I have trouble with. There are times when I am so overwhelmed with loneliness. One night during December 13, our twenty-ninth anniversary, I was so lonely I woke up around two in the morning. I began to pray, which I find myself doing a great deal in the wee hours of the morning. I asked Jesus to go to Wanda and tell her happy anniversary. You know, I immediately had the feeling that she heard my prayer. Jesus said whatever we ask in his name, he will do it. I have a great faith, and I know that Wanda heard my wishes from Jesus. I could also feel the presence of God with me, and it was as if he was wrapping his arms around me and embracing me, as if to say everything is well. I will never forget that feeling, and I have had that same feeling many times since that first night of dire loneliness. I am really not alone. God is always present with me, and I am eternally grateful for that promise he gave me. He never leaves me nor forsakes me, as he promised in Joshua 1:5–6.

Anger is an intense emotional response to situations that are undesirable. Anger has never been a part of my grief stage. A psychologist may say I am not being truthful, but I am. I have been raised to know that when we are born, one day we will die. This life is only a vapor and very short. I know that there is a better place for those who have faith in Jesus Christ, and that place is called heaven. I cannot be angry at my God who has made us and preserved us to live with him eternally. I have never gotten angry at God (or anyone else) for losing my wife. Dying is a natural part of living. When you accept that, you cannot be angry at anyone for a loss. Everyone at one time or another will travel through the pain of losing a loved one. Wanda and I have always placed our faith and trust in Jesus, and we knew that when we died, we would be present with the Lord. I cannot be angry at my God, who has prepared a place for us in heaven. He loves me and all of us. I have always heard that when one looses a spouse the remaining one will either get closer to God or will grow further away from him. I grew closer to God. Anger will only lead to other horrible circumstances and situations in life. So honestly, I have not been angry at God, my family, or others for the loss of my precious wife.

Bargaining is defined as an agreement between parties settling what each shall give and take (or perform and receive) in a transaction. I have not really been involved in this stage either. One does not bargain with God about life or death. I only accept what God hands to me, and I continue to live in faith and trust, according to his plan and love. I have known people who have promised and bargained with God about a health issue, but when it is all over and done with, they usually forget their promise to God. God is not a bargaining chip in order to live longer or shorter. Most people who try to bargain with God usually forget or renege on their bargain. No one should negotiate issues considering life and death. We are to accept life as it is. It is what it is, good or bad. We can pray for God to help us have a better life. The question remains: Do we? Will we? Do we accept that help from God? That is always our individual choice.

Depression is defined as any of these traits: Have you lost interest in things you used to enjoy? Do you avoid being around people, or are you irritated by everyone you are around? Are you feeling intensely sad, down on yourself, or hopeless? Yes, I can say that I was depressed to a certain extent. Depression set in when all my family left after the funeral. I experienced a time where I would cook my food but did not want to eat it or did not want it. I did not have the motivation to eat. I was lonely and felt like the world had swallowed me. I felt that I was in a deep, dark crevice and could not climb out. Other people had said to watch out for depression; they suggested that I try to keep busy. Well, I did all that I could, but that old depression slipped up on me anyway. Finally, I had enough. I very quickly realized that if I were going to survive, it was up to me. I battled it in the only way I knew would work, and that was spiritually. I called out for God to help me and fill me with warm, lasting memories. I looked at some pictures, read a few stories, and came to the conclusion that I must get up, go on, and live life to the fullest. And you know, it worked. I did not even take one antidepressant. Way to go God. Thanks!

Now, when I am depressed, I begin to do things for others. That helps me feel better about myself, and it is like a form of therapy for me. I visit people a great deal in my vocation as a minister, and that helps tremendously. I bake cakes and pies for our Wednesday night meals, and I take some baked items to other people. This also helps me feel like Wanda is nearby, and I begin to hum songs of faith, just like she did when she was happy. I miss that humming in the kitchen so much, but it is a great memory that warms my entire psyche. The battle over depression can be won, but one needs to stick with it and try not to depend upon drugs. We must be careful not to let those drugs become a crutch and fall into a habit. With the help of God on my side, I was able to beat that old depression.

I have seen people who have been so depressed that it chokes the very life out of them. They have no motivation, desires, goals, or ambition to continue living. It is a sad situation when a person falls into a depressed state in life like that. I vowed to God and myself that I would try not to get that depressed. I continue to rest upon the fact of how much my Savior Jesus Christ loves me, and that is enough to get me going. Somehow, God starts a huge, blazing crackling fire under me, and I move very quickly, or else I will get burned very badly. I am glad God has a sense of humor and has given all of us one.

Acceptance is the fact of accepting a situation or another person with their flaws, strengths, and weaknesses. Acceptance of the loss of a spouse is a difficult pill to swallow. I have not yet been able to really and wholeheartedly accept Wanda's death. Perhaps I have, but I cannot get it out of my mind that she is gone. And maybe she does not have to be gone. I am assured that she will always be with me in my memory, and no one can take those memories away from me. Over the almost thirty years that we were married, we had our tussles, fusses, disagreements, and battles. We always made time to iron them out. And speaking of ironing, I did all of that in our married life, as well as use the vacuum cleaner. I did it because I enjoyed it and because I loved it. Come to think of it, I did all the sewing when socks or shirts began suddenly having a hole in them. I loved helping alleviate the load of work so that Wanda could enjoy the simple things in life.

So I guess one could say that at times, I do get stuck in the middle. I suppose that is okay for me, as long as I know how to get out of that situation. I do not wallow in self-pity, nor do I expect anyone else to show that kind of attitude toward me. I simply get up, and as hard as it is at times, I go forward. Wanda would like that. You see, the Children in Action group at church has a motto: "Go forward." That is what I must do each day, and I find that God is strong enough and able to empower me to continue throughout life. Having that power and strength to put one foot in front of the other is a rich and true blessing, only from God. He should not amaze us, but he does all the time, and I am grateful for his amazing grace for me.

When Wanda and I were dating, I took her to Linville Caverns in North Carolina. It was a beautiful place, and we took the tour like a lot of other people that day. At one point, we were the only two people around and got stuck in between two enormous rocks. We had to go through them to get out. We finally wiggled, twisted, and pushed each other, and with a big sigh, we went through the opening. When I experience a little of that old depression, I think of that trip and get to laughing, and I find strength from God to go on. Life is funny, and whether we cry, laugh, or show no expression at all, we must go forward. We went on many trips where we had to go no other direction but forward. This life now is another such time. God has something wonderful, exciting, and life-changing in store for me, and I continue to pray for him to let me know what it is. He may even allow it to fall directly into my lap. God does things like that, you know.

These stages of grief are real. They hurt to the core of one's existence. No one can understand if they have not been in a similar situation. I would sympathize with church members who had lost their loved ones. I ministered at their funerals but had no idea what they were going through. Until I lost my own wife, I did not know all the feelings that I would eventually go through. I always thought that I would be checking out of this world first, since women live longer than men. I guess they do because they are tougher than men are. They keep on working and cleaning when sick, but men act like little babies. Am I not right, men? You bet your bottom dollar I am. I continue to cherish my marriage and life with my wife, and I will never forget her love and support for me as long as I live.

I am sure there are other aspects of grief that I have not covered, but all the stages are difficult to work through. All I can suggest to you is that you should take each day, one day at a time. Some days will be all right, while other days will be rotten. No matter which day you find yourself facing, remember that you can make it through that day. As a Christian, it is imperative that I keep my eyes focused on my Savior. He gives me strength and a reason to keep on going. I am sure that you will continue, but it may not be easy at all. Remember that Jesus gives all of us a reason for living.

Some of the days that I have lived through could be described as "crap-tacular." This means that you have an awful messy day, and it is not at all spectacular. This word was coined by my wonderful wife. Wanda had some of those days at Clean World where she worked until the day she went to be with Jesus in heaven. Clean World was the place where Wanda loved to work. She was the accountant, payroll clerk, made appointments, and handled disagreements. I guess you could have said that she was in quality control. She loved her work and said it was an opportunity to share her faith. Her colleagues called several times to find how she did certain things and how to even get into her computer. She was so concerned a great deal about their faith in Jesus. Wanda lived that faith out in the workplace even when she felt like throwing in the towel.

Another word that Wanda used when things were not going well was "chill ax." This means to chill out and relax at the same time. Some things in life you cannot correct, so do the best you can at what you are doing, roll with the punches, and you will make it. I promise that you will survive. I survived, with a great deal of encouragement from family, friends, and church members. You can control some of the things you go through. Give yourself some credit, and get on with life, even though it is difficult. God will sustain you when you reach out to him. I am living proof of that one astounding fact. As Wanda would say many times, "I'm just saying." She would always say that when she brought a life-changing point to the table. It did make one think and take notice.

Chapter 8

My Public Meltdown

I have been embarrassed by my actions in public. These actions were not at all immoral or unethical. They were truly unexpected, and I was caught off-guard at the time. I had heard other people say that they had at one time or another having a "public meltdown." Rather than this, I believe I had experienced a spinning of the wheels in life. I did not know what to expect or when to expect it. It really sneaks upon you without warning. I do not like the unexpected, especially in my case. The event that triggers a meltdown is usually a very small aspect of life. For me it was, and I happened to fall to pieces in front of some of the most loving and compassionate people in my life. After this spinning of the wheels, I was able to continue with my service to the Lord as his messenger that day.

After the loss of my wife, I heard that I would be tempted to do all kinds of things. That is true, and I fought with all my strength and faith in God to help me run from the temptations that were staring me in my face. I have been tempted to go to bars, get involved with other women, or do drugs or drink alcohol; these things would destroy me and my witness for Jesus Christ. I was able to survive and fight off Satan. I became the winner, and I give God the credit for it all. You see, without Jesus to help me, I would have fallen victim to some of those terrible worldly pleasures.

God has put a hedge around me and protected me from all those temptations. I was able to say no to the schemes of Satan. I did not allow Satan to try to destroy or prevent me from serving my Savior and Lord Jesus Christ... He continues to tempt me, but I have a loving heavenly Father who has given me power over Satan, and I am the victor and conqueror in my own life. Well, so much for the worldly luring factors to get out of the plan of God.

My public meltdown happened all of a sudden. I had been doing well for a few short weeks. The idea of living alone had begun to sink in, and I was making decisions on my own again; although I did not like it, I had to live with it. Making serious and life-changing decisions certainly was not to be expected so soon after my loss, but I could not have equipped myself for what was to come. I always prayed before I made any decision and seemed to make the right choice.

This particular Sunday morning started out to be a very good one. I had gone to open the church earlier than usual. I had a great time of prayer and fellowship with God before everyone else arrived. He had assured me that he would always be at my call and would strengthen me when I needed him to. All the preliminary announcements went well, and the songs that we sung were especially touching. Connie Woodard is our pianist and does a fantastic job each Sunday. Katherine Sumner also does an equally great job each week. Connie and Katherine played a musical duet that really set the mood for the sermon. I started with my introduction to the sermon and I asked everyone to turn to one of the Psalms. I began to read, but when I got to the words, "Hear me O God," I discovered that I could not go on. I became so emotional that I began to cry. I could not focus on the words for the tears in my eyes. God knew my heat and I could not disappoint him. I got it together and began to continue with the sermon. I am so thankful that God empowered me to finish those spiritual truths that I was sharing with the congregation. God continued to bless everyone that day. I truly experienced the presence of God on that very difficult day. Once again, God received the praise for all he does.

The tears were really not tears of grief, but of insurmountable joy from God. The spiritual joy I was experiencing was refreshing and enlightening, to say the least. I spent about five or six minutes looking down at the Bible. As I got myself together, I could see all of my brothers and sisters with their heads bowed, and I knew that they were praying for me. I had a great feeling of defeat and victory, at the same time. I knew that my Christian family loved me and cared deeply for me. I immediately experienced strength from their prayers, and I was able to continue with the sermon. Many people said that the sermon was one of the best they had heard. In my weakness, God was glorified and Jesus was once again lifted up.

I went home after the service, prayed, and asked God why all this happened. I had built up a great deal of emotions, which had to come out. I realized that I was human and that the people needed to see me in my humanity. They saw that their pastor was grieving, but the entire congregation was grieving with me. As I said earlier, this was a spinning of the wheels; like a tractor getting stuck in the mud. I had so many issues going on at one time I was overwhelmed and had to take another long deep breath. This loss for me and the church was too sudden and unexpected. Perhaps we as Christians should expect the unexpected when it comes to trusting, believing, serving, and following God. He sure threw me for a loop, but I continued to remain faithful to him in all things. I have been growing closer to God more than ever before in my life. God has truly been my strength and fortress in my life.

After my public meltdown, or spinning wheels, whichever you prefer, I have had other incidents that I gave glory to God for. As I let all this emotion out, I realized that I was beginning to heal. If I were to keep these emotions inside of me, I would pop like a balloon. That would not be good for me or the people around me. This letting go, if you will, helped me see my true and pressing situation in life. Allowing my emotions to flow freely enabled me to discover more of God's abundant blessings.

Those blessings from God help us become more mature in our faith. I have discovered through my sleepless nights that God always listens to us. He always answers our prayers, sometimes immediately. He comforts us beyond all our expectation. God shows us the way to travel, even when we lose our way in the dark of night. God is an ever-present help, and he always has a listening ear. I have begun to pray for Jesus to come back each day. I did not pray that until I lost my wife. My prayers are different now. Usually, when Wanda and I would read the Bible, we would take turns praying. Sometimes, the prayers would be for very specific situations, and at other times, they would be much more general in nature. Sometimes, we would pray for the Children in Action group; their prayer concerns would include a gold fish, Grandpa's leg, a school teacher, an aunt who was sick, or someone to accept Jesus as Savior. We prayed for all these concerns each night. Many of them were filled with great stories, and we were delighted to be able to pray for these children's concerns. Children and their concept of prayer is so simple. I wish that Christian adults would get it like children do.

When I pray in a restaurant, people often make comments, and I take that as an opportunity to minister. But in some cases, I was still dealing with my grief. It seemed difficult to get in touch with God because of my grief-stricken days. However, God always pulled through for me, and I continued sharing how wonderful God has been to me. That initial public meltdown led to times of discovery as well as rediscovery in my life. I was in a position to attentively sit and hear what God had to say to me. Remarkably enough, God told me that it would be all right, that all this was a part of life, and that I would become a stronger person and a better Christian as a result of my deep loss. At that time, it was very difficult to understand this message from God. But I knew that God would never lead me in the wrong direction or guide me in the dark.

After examining my public meltdown, I discovered that I had little episodes of meltdowns throughout the day. They helped me realize that I am continuing to deal with all the emotions and decisions that I make each day. One example was the first time I went to the cardiologist for a checkup after Wanda died. For some reason, all my paperwork had to be filled out again. I did not expect what was to come. I struggled with some of the questions knowing they had to be answered. Everything was going well until the question of marital status came up. For the first time in my life, I had to circle "W" for "widower." I fell to pieces in the waiting room. I sobbed for about ten minutes, and then the nurse called me back to see the doctor. She asked what was wrong, and I told her. This was not a good day for me at all, and I did not want to explain everything over and over again.

To say the least, the office visit was very brief, and I went back home. All that afternoon, I could do nothing but sob and recall all the things Wanda and I did together; they were so much fun. I finally survived that day, and the next day was a little better for me.

You see, in all of these emotions, evaluations, continuing grief, and regrouping, God has never once left me alone. He was always with me to encourage me and strengthen me along the path of live. In June, a dear friend of mine, Rev. Thomas McLean, who is the pastor of a nearby church, lost his wife to a massive heart attack. They were eating at Shoney's, and she slumped over; that was it. Like Wanda, she was only fifty-four years of age. I went to the hospital in Hartsville to minister to him. I knew exactly what he was desperately going through. I knew the pain and sorrow of losing a partner and loving wife. All four of us had gone to Southeastern Seminary in Wake Forest, North Carolina, and we were great friends. Strange how things happen in life, is it not? All this brought back my personal pain and sorrow, but I helped Thomas try to cope with what had happened.

Today, Thomas is having a very difficult time dealing with his situation and he is moving on in life. It is hard to do, but God gives us grace, love, and understanding, and his presence helps us to forge ahead. We have the hope of knowing that we will see them in heaven. It may be sooner than any of us realize, according to the situation in this world.

Other small meltdowns come when people find out what happened. I try to keep myself together, but it all comes back, as if I am reliving all the emotions over again. I simply go with the flow now. If I tear up some, the people try to understand. For the most part, I ask for God to give me strength to endure; he always pulls me through, and I am grateful for that. I started to look at some pictures the other day but could not bring myself to see them. The pain continued to hurt so much so I put the pictures back in the living room end tables. Perhaps these small meltdowns will always be a part of my life. I will try, as the Brits say, to keep a stiff upper lip and go on, with Wanda always in my heart and memory. I will never forget her.

There are still times I catch myself calling out to Wanda when I come back from my morning walk or coming back from a busy day of visiting. She would always welcome me back into our home as if I had been away for several days. Whenever I had to drive to the hospital in Florence, she would make me call her when I arrived. I always promised to call her to say that I got there all right. I really do miss that, and at times, I have found myself calling her cell phone. Oh, how I wish at times I could speak to her and tell her how things are going in life. Little things like that were so special, and I miss them so much.

Small task's like washing Chip, our dog, was a difficult chore, but Wanda would "woman-handle" him and put him in a headlock while washing his face. It would be my pleasure to wash the rest of him while she held him. Now I have to do all that by myself, but it gets done. Things like shopping for clothes or eating out often make me cry. Those are the things that allow the tears to come, but I am glad that they do come. Yes, I continue to catch myself and find that she is not here for me to touch or hold her hand. Even though I have her in my memory and in my heart, it is not the same as seeing her and talking to her throughout the day. Many times, Wanda would call me from her office and ask how I was doing or see if I wanted to meet her for supper at the Mayflower, Joe's, or Takis. We often did this, but not anymore. I go alone now and remember the good conversations we would have. Going it alone at times is terrible, but I often see someone I know, and we talk and remember the good old days with the love of my life.

I shall never forget the first time I set eyes on Wanda. I knew that I was going to marry her. I had to sternly convince her of the idea, and she finally accepted the invitation to become my wife. One could say that it was love at first sight—for me, at least. It still is, even though she is in heaven now. Wanda always wore very nice clothes that her mother made. She always looked her best whenever I saw her while we were dating and at other times. She was everything a man would want in a woman. I had great respect for her and her belief in Jesus as Lord and Savior of her life; I also admired her strong work ethic. Wanda was so proud of me throughout the years, and I was proud of her. She helped me work on my doctorate at Gardner-Webb University and could have earned the degree herself, for putting up with me and reading all of my papers. Wanda was a great support and challenged me to work hard and make the best of each day I had. I continue to make the best of each day that God has given me.

Wanda and I always had the idea, and prayed to leave this world together, hand in hand, as Jesus came to split the eastern sky open. We often talked about how happy that would be for so many people (and how sad it would be for many more). It did not happen the way we wanted, but she is waiting on me, and I will see her later in heaven. I have that promise from Jesus, and I know that I will be reunited with her and other family members who are awaiting our arrival. What a joyous time that will be, to walk through the gates of heaven and see Jesus face-to-face. I can hardly wait to see him and tell him how thankful I am for giving his life for me, so that I can live with him eternally. What a happy time that will be when my Jesus I shall see.

John tells us of many sights he sees in heaven described in the book of Revelation. He tells of the streets of gold, the gasper walls, crystal clear river from the throne of God, and the pearl gates at the entrance. All of these and numerous other blessings are waiting for those who love and serve our awesome Savior

Jesus Christ. Just imagine this. Having a body that will never grow old; having no aches and pains will be exciting for us. Can you imagine when all those people see, hear, and speak for the first time. Wow! What a blessing that is in store for those people. It makes me almost homesick and wanting to go to the other side; our heavenly home.

Chapter 9

God Loves Me: I Am Not Alone

Back in my formative years, I remember going to Piney Knob Baptist Church for Vacation Bible School. This church was in Shingle Hollow, North Carolina, near our home. We had a different flavor of cool-aide drink and big round cookies each night (refreshments sure have changed in today's Bible school). I learned that Jesus loves me. We sang "Jesus Loves Me" almost every night. We had to memorize scriptures from the Bible, and on family night, we recited our memory verses. We all felt so proud. Those hot summer weeks of Vacation Bible School were a thrill. This was where I first heard that Jesus loved me so much that he gave his life so that I could live forever with him. It was not until later, at the age of sixteen, that I gave my life to Jesus and was baptized. I immediately began to pray for God's direction to know what he wanted me to do. About a year later, I heard a still small voice say, "Preach." I have been doing so ever since 1976. I have not regretted it at all. Preaching gives me joy to share the Good News of Jesus Christ.

There are so many Bible verses about God's love. I will share some of those that have really moved me to a deeper relationship with my Savior Jesus Christ. After all, it is not about denomination; it is about a relationship with Jesus as Savior of our lives and Lord of our possessions. He must be both Lord and Savior of our lives.

Throughout the horrible loss of my wife, I thought I was alone. But in the wee hours of the morning, feeling all alone, I began to grow a deeper relationship with our heavenly Father. I had some very special and intimate talks with my God. Through Jesus going to God, I realized that I was not at all alone. I realized again and again that my Jesus loves me. On one occasion, I found myself singing very quietly, "Jesus Loves Me." I have known this all along in my life, and the love of God really swept over me and went down deep into my innermost being. I am truly blessed because I have Jesus in my heart and soul; regardless of what happens I am never alone by Christ's standards. I must keep this in mind at all times in my life.

The scriptures that I will share with you have helped me battle loneliness and separation, and they allowed me to regain strength from our heavenly father, who lives in those who have a deep growing relationship with him through Jesus Christ. I am joyous in the fact that I have the greatest source of literature, called the Bible, to help me find eternal assurance in the fact that God continues to care for me and love me. Not only do I have God who loves me, I have a loving Savior Jesus Christ, a loving family, and Christian friends who pray for me constantly.

I would like to begin with the Psalms and share a few of these that have helped me go forward into the unknown, with Christ holding my hand. I know that Christ has often been carrying me along the way.

> May the LORD answer you in the day of trouble; May the name of the God of Jacob defend you; May He send you help from the sanctuary, And strengthen you out

of Zion; May He remember all your offerings, And accept your burnt sacrifice. Selah. May He grant you according to your heart's *desire,* And fulfill all your purpose. We will rejoice in your salvation, And in the name of our God we will set up *our* banners! May the LORD fulfill all your petitions. Now I know that the LORD saves His anointed; He will answer him from His holy heaven With the saving strength of His right hand. Some *trust* in chariots, and some in horses; But we will remember the name of the LORD our God. They have bowed down and fallen; But we have risen and stand upright. Save, LORD! May the King answer us when we call (Psalm 20:1-9).

Oh, taste and see that the LORD *is* good; Blessed *is* the man *who* trusts in Him! Oh, fear the LORD, you His saints! *There is* no want to those who fear Him. The young lions lack and suffer hunger; But those who seek the LORD shall not lack any good *thing. The righteous* cry out, and the LORD hears, And delivers them out of all their troubles. The LORD *is* near to those who have a broken heart, And saves such as have a contrite spirit. Many *are* the afflictions of the righteous, But the LORD delivers him out of them all (Psalm 34:8–10, 17–19).

I will extol You, my God, O King; And I will bless Your name forever and ever. Every day I will bless You, And I will praise Your name forever and ever. Great *is* the LORD, and greatly to be praised; And His greatness *is* unsearchable. One generation shall praise Your works to another, And shall declare Your mighty acts. I will meditate on the glorious splendor of Your majesty,

And on Your wondrous works. *Men* shall speak of the might of Your awesome acts, And I will declare Your greatness. They shall utter the memory of Your great goodness, And shall sing of Your righteousness. The LORD *is* gracious and full of compassion, Slow to anger and great in mercy. The LORD *is* good to all, And His tender mercies *are* over all His works. All Your works shall praise You, O LORD, And Your saints shall bless You. They shall speak of the glory of Your kingdom, And talk of Your power, To make known to the sons of men His mighty acts, And the glorious majesty of His kingdom. Your kingdom *is* an everlasting kingdom, And Your dominion *endures* throughout all generations. The LORD upholds all who fall, And raises up all *who are* bowed down. The eyes of all look expectantly to You, And You give them their food in due season. You open Your hand And satisfy the desire of every living thing. The LORD *is* righteous in all His ways, Gracious in all His works. The LORD *is* near to all who call upon Him, To all who call upon Him in truth. He will fulfill the desire of those who fear Him; He also will hear their cry and save them. The LORD preserves all who love Him, But all the wicked He will destroy. My mouth shall speak the praise of the LORD, And all flesh shall bless His holy name Forever and ever (Psalm 145:1-21).

These special psalms are helping to fill the void in my heart and soul. It is so wonderful when God speaks to us as we read his word. I am constantly refueled with the assurance and direction that God gives me while reading and studying these truths of God. I have gained abundant strength from these gentle and compassionate words of God, from the depths of David's heart to my heart. As we face loss in our lives as Christians, we must reach into the nuggets of truth and light that are found in God's word. These nuggets of truth help guide us and guard us from the evil dealings of Satan, and we find that we are truly over comers and conquerors in this world. There are many other psalms that have helped me, and I rediscover them each day. I must remember that God's mercies are new every morning for me.

Here are some more scriptures that have given me boldness and strength to continue living; I am grateful to have these eternal sources from the very heart of God:

> Let not your heart be troubled; you believe in God, believe also in Me. In My Father's house are many mansions; if *it were* not *so,* I would have told you. I go to prepare a place for you. And if I go and prepare a place for you, I will come again and receive you to Myself; that where I am, *there* you may be also. And where I go you know, and the way you know." Thomas said to Him, "Lord, we do not know where You are going, and how can we know the way?" Jesus said to him, "I am the way, the truth, and the life. No one comes to the Father except through Me" (John 14:1–6).

> Therefore, having been justified by faith, we have peace with God through our Lord Jesus Christ, through whom also we have access by faith into this grace in which we stand, and rejoice in hope of the glory of God. And not only *that,* but we also glory in tribulations, knowing that tribulation produces perseverance; and perseverance, character; and character, hope. Now hope does not disappoint, because the love of God has been

poured out in our hearts by the Holy Spirit who was given to us (Romans 5:1–5).

Paul, an apostle of Jesus Christ by the will of God, and Timothy *our* brother, To the church of God which is at Corinth, with all the saints who are in all Achaia: Grace to you and peace from God our Father and the Lord Jesus Christ. Blessed *be* the God and Father of our Lord Jesus Christ, the Father of mercies and God of all comfort, who comforts us in all our tribulation, that we may be able to comfort those who are in any trouble, with the comfort with which we ourselves are comforted by God (2 Corinthians 1:1–4).

Finally, my brethren, be strong in the Lord and in the power of His might. Put on the whole armor of God, that you may be able to stand against the wiles of the devil. For we do not wrestle against flesh and blood, but against principalities, against powers, against the rulers of the darkness of this age, against spiritual *hosts* of wickedness in the heavenly *places*. Therefore take up the whole armor of God, that you may be able to withstand in the evil day, and having done all, to stand. Stand therefore, having girded your waist with truth, having put on the breastplate of righteousness, and having shod your feet with the preparation of the gospel of peace; above all, taking the shield of faith with which you will be able to quench all the fiery darts of the wicked one. And take the helmet of salvation, and the sword of the Spirit, which is the word of God; praying always with all prayer and supplication in the Spirit, being watchful to this end with all perseverance and supplication for all the saints— and for me, that utterance may be given to me, that I may open my mouth boldly to make known the mystery of the gospel, for which I am an ambassador in chains; that in it I may speak boldly, as I ought to speak (Ephesians 6:10–20).

Therefore humble yourselves under the mighty hand of God, that He may exalt you in due time, casting all your care upon Him, for He cares for you. Be sober, be vigilant; because your adversary the devil walks about like a roaring lion, seeking whom he may devour. Resist him, steadfast in the faith, knowing that the same sufferings are experienced by your brotherhood in the world. But may the God of all grace, who called us to His eternal glory by Christ Jesus, after you have suffered a while, perfect, establish, strengthen, and settle *you*. To Him *be* the glory and the dominion forever and ever. Amen (1 Peter 5:6–10).

These scriptures above have encouraged me, inspired me, and redirected my life in such a way that I have been refreshed in the love, guidance, and power of God. Without these instructions, and the leadership of the Holy Spirit, I would have fallen victim to Satan's alluring schemes that keep Christians from being productive in life. Those schemes could have destroyed my life, but God always comes through for his people, and he came through for me at just the right time. Glory to God for his unchanging and penetrating word of truth and grace! In difficult times of our lives, God always has direction for us to follow. This direction is always the right path in which to travel, and we know it will lead us to our eternal rewards of seeing him face-to-face.

Hebrews 13:35-6 gives me great strength and courage; it tells me that God is always going to be with me and that nothing can harm me as long as I follow him:

> Let your conduct be without covetousness; be content with such things as you have. For He Himself has said, "I will never leave you nor forsake you." So we may boldly say: "The LORD is my helper; I will not fear. What can man do to me?"

Each day, I rest upon this fact: that God is hearing my prayers and that he is keeping me safe in his compassionate arms. Sometimes, that becomes so overwhelming, all I can do is praise God for his awesome presence. I know beyond a shadow of a doubt that I am not alone and that one day, I will be with Jesus and all the family members who have become eternal citizens of heaven.

Another Old Testament scripture comes to mind in our weakest moments and to remind us that God continues to come to our rescue. In Isaiah 40:31, we read these words: "But those who wait on the LORD Shall renew *their* strength; They shall mount up with wings like eagles, They shall run and not be weary, They shall walk and not faint." I have found this to be all too often true for those who follow God's perfect and complete design for their lives. In our weakest moments, it is God who empowers us and gives us the extra thrust to keep on living the life that he wants us to live.

In Philippians 4:13, these victorious words were spoken from Paul, who knew what it meant to be with much in life and with so little: "I can do all things through Christ who strengthens me." I know now that I can continue living my life for my Savior Jesus Christ and that life nor death, nor anything that we face will separate us from the amazing love of God through Jesus Christ. As a Christian, I must continue to find the spiritual fortitude to continue serving my wonderful God, no matter what may come my way. I have been through the fire and have come out unscathed, by the grace of God. I have survived by the ever-present hand of God in my life, and I will praise him forevermore. He is worthy to be praised.

I stated in the beginning of my struggles that I always envisioned Wanda and I going up to heaven together, hand in hand. What a wonderful way to go. Well, that did not happen as I thought, but she jumped the gun on me. I pray every day for the return of our Savior, when the eastern sky breaks forth, and he puts his foot out and calls us to be with him in heaven forever. What a great trumpet sound when we hear it. For many Christians, it will be a glorious time, but not so for the lost who are left behind. I look forward to that day, when my Jesus I shall see. I continue to live as God would have me to. I try tirelessly, with God's help, to continuously seek his direction through the greatest avenue that we as Christians have, and that is prayer.

Prayer for me is so simple. We surrender to God and ask, in deep abiding faith, becoming obedient to him as he answers our petitions that we place before him. We have no room in our hearts to doubt, for doubt comes from Satan, the evil one. In Matthew 7:7–8, we have it stated very simply by our Savior Jesus Christ. He says, "Ask, and it will be given to you; seek, and you will find; knock, and it will be opened to you. For everyone who asks receives, and he who seeks finds, and to him who knocks it will be opened." See how simple prayer is? But we must ask in complete and unwavering faith. When we believe in this type of faith and thank Jesus for answering those prayers in advance, he will assuredly answer them. We must have immovable faith in him.

For thousands of years, faithful men and women have prayed for God to intervene in life's situations. Every prayer that has been prayed has been answered in the way God intends. It is a good thing that God is in control of answering our prayers and not us. We certainly would make a mess out of things if it were up to us. Considering the ministry of prayer from Chrysostom, the archbishop of Constantinople gives us these thoughts:

> The potency of prayer hath subdued the strength of fire; it had bridled the rage of lions, hushed the anarchy of rest, extinguished wars, appeased the elements, expelled demons, burst the chains of death, expanded the gates of heaven, assuaged diseases, repelled frauds, rescued cities from destruction, stayed the sun it its course, and arrested the progress of the thunderbolt.
>
> Prayer is an all-efficient panoply, a treasure undiminished, a mine which is never exhausted, a sky unobscured by clouds, a heaven unruffled by the storm. It is the root, the fountain, the mother of a thousand blessings.[1]

Chrysostom was right in stating all that prayer is and can doing. Although it does all this and more, we must remember who we are praying to. We must remember that our awesome God will hear our prayers and answer them. There is no obstacle that stands in our way from praying, except our own wills. We must also be careful in what we pray for, for when we get our request answered, it is too late to say, "I did not mean that, God."

---

[1] E.M. Bounds, *Power Through Prayer: Purpose in Prayer* (Westwood, New Jersey: Barbour & Company, 1984), 25.

If it were not for God's mercy, I would not be able to continue to function in life. I always need God to guide me, listen to me, understand me, and empower me to participate in growing the kingdom of Christ. I have answered the greatest call in the entire world from the creator of the universe, and I desire in my heart to please God in all I do. God's mercy has been a daily staple in my life, especially now that I am single again. John Wesley says this about prayer and what we gain in prayer: "Bear up the hands that hang down, by faith and prayer; support the tottering knees. Have you any days of fasting and prayer? Storm the throne of grace and persevere therein, and mercy will come down."[2] I have found that this is true at any time of the day or even in the wee hours of the morning. God will listen to our prayers, and his mercy will come flowing down like a torrent in the springtime. These refreshing moments of unmerited grace and mercy come when we think there is no hope or rescue. Yet again, God always amazes me in all he does in life.

When we pray in the name of Jesus, we do not realize what power and strength we have. At the name of Jesus, every knee will bow and tongue will confess him as Savior and Lord. Things happen and situations change, and people's lives are transformed at the name of Jesus. The greatest name in all the world is Jesus, and one day, he is coming back to get his people, and we are going to have a "Holy Hallelujah Hoedown." This will be like we have never seen before.

What's in a name? I say everything, if we look close enough. C. H. Spurgeon says it well:

> Lord Jesus, cause me to know in my daily experience the glory and sweetness of Thy name, and then teach me how to use it in my prayer, so that I may be even

---

[2] Bounds, *Power Through Prayer*, 75.

like Israel, a prince prevailing with God. Thy name is my passport, and secures me access; Thy name is my plea, and secures me answer; Thy name is my honour and secures me glory. Blessed Name, Thou are honey in my mouth, music in my ear, heaven in my heart, and all in all to my being![3]

Yes, Jesus is the sweetest name I know, and I know that I can call upon him many times, and he will answer me. He never says to call him back, leave a message, or send an email, blog or even text. He immediately hears and answers. No questions asked. He listens attentively.

One night in December 2015, I rolled over in bed, but Wanda was not there for me to touch. I was very lonely. It was our twenty-ninth wedding anniversary. I was a mess. I needed to be held and wanted to tell Wanda happy anniversary so badly. My broken heart cried out to Jesus, and he heard me and said, "Bill, it is done." I felt his embrace and warmth down deep in my soul. I literally felt the arms of Jesus hugging me so tight that night. This came only by prayer and being broken, but also by being put back together by the Master Potter, Jesus. This was a major breakthrough for me, and I began to see my Savior in a more intimate level. Jesus truly is my all-in-all in life. Without Jesus, I could not have functioned throughout the ordeal of losing my precious wife. Jesus is truly the best friend I have. He listens to me when no one else has time or seems to care. I praise Jesus for being my Savior and Lord of my life.

I have been praying and speaking to God through Jesus more than ever. If you live long enough, you will experience a tragedy in your life. The only way that I survived was to use those lonely, heartbroken hours talking to Jesus. He heard every

---

[3] Bounds, *Purpose in Prayer*, 125.

prayer that I prayed. I have no doubt about that fact. When you pour out your heart and soul to God, he performs wonderful acts of love and comfort. There is nothing as refreshing and enlightening as the comfort and understanding of our heavenly Father. Prayer has always been an important aspect of ministry. I could not have ministered if I did not pray seeking for God's guidance and the leadership of the Holy Spirit. I have always prayed about any and all situations. I pray as I drive in the vehicle going from house to house or hospital to hospital. Get this and do not forget it: God always hears your prayers, and he always answers them. Just be careful what you ask for; you may get it. After you pray for it and receive it, then it is too late to give it back. You must be serious, intentional, and specific about the issues and people you pray for. You must have total confidence that God will answer your prayers. There is no space in our intention for doubt.

God loves me so much, and I am not alone, as some people might think. I rest on the fact of the truth of the scriptures that tell me what Jesus said in Revelation 22:20–21: "He who testifies to these things says, 'Surely I am coming quickly.' Amen. Even so, come, Lord Jesus! The grace of our Lord Jesus Christ be with you all. Amen." I do not know about you, but I welcome the fact that Jesus is coming soon. We do not know when that will be; only God does.

All I know is that I am ready for his glorious coming, and I will be taken up with him to my new mansion in heaven. This fact is really the only one that we can count on. Someone said we can count on two things in life: death and taxes. For Christians, we do not really die; we only begin to live eternally in heaven with our Lord and Savior Jesus Christ. Do you get that fact?

Just think: no more trials, tribulations, worries, heartaches, fighting, poverty, social injustice, discrimination, sickness, and yes, no more death. Now when you begin to think of all the benefits of heaven; it really is worth the life we live, all because of Jesus. Total and complete rest will be awaiting us, as will relaxation, and praising our Savior and creator throughout all eternity. Kind of makes me homesick; I want to go now. By the way, I have been praying each day for Jesus to come back and take us out of this evil and cruel world. One of the most pressing decisions you will make is to give your heart to Jesus and have the assurance that you will journey to heaven, either when the trumpet sounds or God calls you and me home. Either way, it will be a celebratory time, with our souls eternally in heaven with our loved ones and King Jesus with us.

The older one gets the more we may anticipate seeing Jesus. For the Christian this will be a wonderful event. As time goes by, a person realizes that all of their loved ones and friends are in heaven. That makes heaven a sweeter place and it weighs heavier on our souls. I am so glad that God prepared heaven for those who have been faithful to his cause through Jesus Christ. God does not give us the good, or what is better; God gives us the best. If you are a Christian I am sure that you will agree with me on that aspect in life. Even though we may be in the valley; we are only in the valley for a short time. That is one of the many reasons heaven has become sweeter to me in these past months. Weeping and sorrow may endure for a night, but joy comes in the morning. I am living proof of that. My faith has allowed me to prove that point.

Chapter 10

Countless Struggles, God's Work Goes On

There will always be struggles in life. Challenges and difficulties are always a part of life no matter whether you are married or single. When I was married to Wanda, we had many struggles. One of the most difficult ones was not being able to have children. And believe you me, this was very difficult time for both of us. Through prayer and God's guidance, we were able to be content with what God allowed to transpire through his permissive will. By not having children, we were able to help many through ministry opportunities; we helped supply some of the needs their parents could not meet. It would have been a blessing to have children I could talk to and embrace after going through such as loss. Jesus told us that we would have struggles, but we are to make the best of them. When these struggles begin to consume you, then you cease to be a functioning human being. God does not want that to occur at all.

Through many emotional days and nights, without warning, I would feel as if I had been completely swallowed by the great abyss. Just when I thought that this occurred, God allowed a Bible verse to come to my mind. I love the way that

God allows our souls to receive the hope and assurance from his eternal words. One verse that would constantly come to mind and heart was Psalm 30:5, which says, "For His anger *is but for* a moment, His favor *is for* life; Weeping may endure for a night, But joy *comes* in the morning."

I thought I would never stop crying due to my grief and loss. I wondered if I was ever going to get back to normal, if there was a normal. As soon as I thought I had it all together and things were getting better for me, some small thought would enter my heart, and I would get all emotional again. I knew that this would be expected to happen, but I hated the fact that it would happen at the most inopportune times. I would dry my tears away and try to smile, yet down deep inside, I was screaming at the top of my lungs. I would be comforted by the gospel songs I would hear on the satellite radio station in my truck. This usually occurred when I was driving to someone's home to make a visit. God was allowing me to grieve, but at the same time, I was healing. I wanted the healing to hurry; I wanted to get back to a normal life. But then again, I do not believe that there is a normal to anyone's life. We just learn to roll with the punches of life.

Those chores such as doing the laundry, cooking meals, cleaning house, paying the bills, and a number of other tasks are more difficult because we would always do them together. Now, it is just me against the world. Excuse me: It is God and me against the world, or so it seems. You know, God has never let me down at all. Jesus has always been within me and all around me. Jesus is my all-in-all. I have learned even more that time is so precious. I have been reading God's word more and praying to my Savior more than any time in my life. I believe that this is a great attribute, and I am growing ever closer to our heavenly Father in the process. That is what it is: All this stuff is a process in life. We are only promised this hour, and we must make the best of it. If God blesses us with the entire day, then we must make it count as best we can. This stuff is for the Christian a lifestyle of faith, belief, and commitment; to go even deeper, it is what I call total surrender. The only way I could have survived is through the love and care of my Savior Jesus Christ. You see, God did a great miracle when he gave up his only begotten son to die on the cross for us. I do not know about you, but I want to put my arms around him when I get to heaven and tell him how much I love and thank him for dying on the cross for me. Without Jesus in my life, I could be in the gutter (and thank God I am not).

At times, getting out of bed is a struggle for me. Sometime I feel like I am in a lifting fog and I cannot see my way around. Other times I can see clearly and then get pulled back into the fog. Life is a great effort, a labor, something I want to resist. These are struggles because I have the entire house to myself. I no longer sing in the shower, like I used to do. I would often wake Wanda, who loved to sleep into the double digits very late on Saturday mornings. I guess she was penned as a "Night Owl" of sorts. We were the total opposites as far as sleep patterns but so much alike in many other respects. I am so thankful to God for allowing us to remember certain memories. Those I have cherished have helped me make it through each day. There are times when I recall a special memory, and I feel as though I am holding Wanda's hand again, and I begin to laugh, and all of a sudden, I find myself crying once again. But soon thereafter, God places sweet peace in my heart; the joy he gives truly overflows in my soul. I am thankful to God and will praise him evermore.

I have gone through many unexpected struggles in such a short amount of time. I know that I will continue to go through more struggles, but I know that despite those struggles, I must press on and run the race before me. I want it to be said of me, as Paul tells us in Hebrews 12:1–2:

> Therefore we also, since we are surrounded by so great a cloud of witnesses, let us lay aside every weight, and the sin which so easily ensnares *us*, and let us run with endurance the race that is set before us, looking unto Jesus, the author and finisher of *our* faith, who for the joy that was set before Him endured the cross, despising the shame, and has sat down at the right hand of the throne of God.

I want to have run the race of faith. As the clouds of witnesses watch me, I know that they are cheering me and other Christians on in this race. We all must lay aside the entanglements of this world, and we must run for Christ with all of our might and every ounce of strength. Share his love, forgiveness, acceptance, and assurance that we as Christians have that only comes by possessing Jesus in our hearts and souls. Jesus is our author and the finisher of our faith, and he counted it all joy to go through all he did so that we can live with him again in heaven. I will continue to run the race that is before me, even in the midst of persecution, heartache, pain, disgruntled people, grudge-holders, and unforgiving people. I will continue to receive encouragement from those who cheer me on, and I will cheer them on at the same time. Jesus gives us eternal joy as we follow his call. The call to preach that I received from God through Jesus, and by the power of the Holy Spirit, is just as strong as it was when I received it at sixteen years of age. God has much more for me to struggle with, and I will struggle with him on my side. He empowers and enlightens me to do his will each day of my life. What I have is not just a call; it is a lifelong passion to serve God, whenever and wherever he leads.

I am reminded of the call of Noah, Moses, Samuel, Joseph, Isaiah, Jeremiah, Jonah, Habakkuk, Hosea, the disciples, Paul, Timothy, and our precious Savior Jesus Christ. All of these men were serving our heavenly Father. One gave his life so that we could live with him eternally. I am in good company. If you are called to serve Christ in any capacity, then you too are in good company. We must go forward and run the race with great enthusiasm and excitement, for there are many souls to win for the kingdom of Christ.

These men had their own struggles and barreled through obstacles of unbelief, skepticism, and hatred, and yet they completed faithfully their race. They won with a great deal of celebration. They made it to the finish line and celebrated, for they accomplished their specific mission in the world. Those struggles, if anything, made them all better men of God. When we rely upon God to lead us through the stormy blasts of life, we know that whatever he leads us to, he will lead us through. That is Good News to all people. God has led me to a difficult part of my life, and he is leading me through that difficulty. I celebrate the fact that he has not given up on me, nor will he give up on me. We will always be a work in progress. He has wonderful things to accomplish in life for all of his people, as we struggle along the journey of our faith. We can see the finish line; we are too close to turn back now. We must go forward with all our might and finish the race before us, as the great cloud of witnesses look on.

Throughout my life, I find that each day is totally different from the day before. I am glad that life is like that. If each day were the same, then life would not be worth living. I am glad that God adds some spice and challenge to our lives each day. The other day, I was cooking for the week, and the doorbell rang. I did not want to be disturbed, but I went to the door anyway to see who it was. It was a visitor I really did not want to see at the time, as I wanted to finish my tasks. I invited him in and we spoke for about an hour; the conversation was more pleasant than I could have ever dreamed. God took a dreaded visit and turned it into a blessing for me and for the other person. God is great, all the time.

These struggles may throw us for a loop; they will take us either closer to or further away from God. I have chosen in my life to allow all these struggles to lead me closer to God, as he understands me, loves me, directs me, and protects me each day. People cannot even fathom the issues, complaints, situations, and concerns that a minister hears, unless they are blessed to be called to that service. Ministers desire to see all the congregation work together and live in unity and harmony as we share the Gospel of Jesus Christ. There are times when ministers feel like throwing in the towel, but God always allows them to be encouraged by some small blessing. It is Satan's job and purpose to discourage all Christians.

We must realize that we are stronger than Satan will ever be, according to 1 John 4:4, which says, "You are of God, little children, and have overcome them, because He who is in you is greater than he who is in the world." God, who is within you and me through Jesus our Savior, is greater than Satan, who is the prince of the power of the air in the world. We must believe that truth from God's word and realize where our power comes from. It comes from Almighty God, who lives and breathes within us as Christians. Nothing is impossible with God. Matthew 19:26 tells us a nugget of truth to follow in life: "But Jesus looked at *them* and said to them, "With men this is impossible, but with God all things are possible." Jesus said all things are possible. When he said this, he meant that *all* things are possible with him. The fact remains in us that we must believe what Jesus said is true and applicable to our lives.

God's work will continue, with us or without us. The point is that God does not need us; we so desperately need God in our lives. We need God to help us make it through the difficult circumstances we face each day. When we allow God to use us for his glory and adoration, then he takes delight in his people. Do you and I take delight in the fact that God may use us today to get his purpose to the people? No matter what loss we have had in life, if we allow God to use us, he can and will do miraculous things in our lives. We must trust, try, and prove him, and he will always come through for us. I have said before that whatever God leads us to, he will lead us through. That is a wonderful thought. We should not ever sweat the small stuff in life. When we leave it all up to God and do our part, then he will do wonders in our presence.

Since the loss of Wanda, I have really rediscovered the meaning of the presence of God. He is always available to hear what we have to say. He is seen as a gentle rain drop, a fluttering bird, a soothing breeze, and an eerie silence. It does not matter what God may be seen as; he is always near and even within our complex yet gentle souls. Make room for God and especially his Son Jesus Christ. Jesus surely made room at the cross for you and me to accept him as Savior. We must make room in our souls for Jesus. We can never get enough of Jesus. He is more than salvation for us. The more we study the Bible and get deeper each day, the more we find out how much God truly loves us. I am so glad that he does not discard us like we do yesterday's newspaper. I am glad that God loves us and is ready to forgive us when we call upon him. He desires a thriving relationship with each of us.

God's presence with me is indescribable at times. I can feel him more than ever. It is like he is stuck close to me, and I love that. I know that he is seeing and hearing all that I encounter in life. This is a comforting thought, and I draw a great deal of strength from it. Knowing that God always allows the best to come to us brings a new perspective in our lives. Bad things do happen at times, but God always turns them into a great blessing. That is what happened to Joseph, who was sold into slavery, and later, God took that evil situation and saved his family from extinction. God always has our best interests at heart.

The other week, a hurricane came through the state of South Carolina. In our area of Darlington County, the wind was fierce, and the rain came down in torrents. During this time, I again realized how powerful and awesome our God is. Throughout the evening and the next day, I took an opportunity to catch up on some reading. At times, the wind was so violent that it made me wonder if the house was going to disintegrate. During those violent howling winds, I found myself putting down my book and quietly praying for God's protective care. When your house begins to squeak, pop, and crack, you wonder if you are going to fly away, like Dorothy in *The Wizard of Oz*. As time went on, the rain and wind subsided, and everything was all right with the house. God yet again sustained us, and we weathered the storm. I continued praying until the storm passed by and gave God the praise for safety.

During my struggles and heartaches, God always helps me weather the storms that I face. Those storms help me to gain a new perspective on life and gain a better, clearer understanding of who God is to me. As I have said many times, God is my all-in-all in life. Without him, I do not know what I would do. I cannot imagine a person or family going through a storm in life, such as losing a family member, without God in their lives.

I continue to thank God for his wonderful abiding presence in my life, throughout the difficult episodes I face. When we hold onto God's hands, he always carries us through in life. It will be a glorious event when we see God face-to-face. Then, and only then, we will have no more storms in life to trip us up. How glorious is that to think about?

Some televangelist predicted that the Antichrist would appear before or around December of 2016. If that actually happens, then I pray the rapture of the church takes place soon. Now you talk about some stirring and changing of things; it will happen in the twinkling of an eye: "In a moment, in the twinkling of an eye, at the last trumpet. For the trumpet will sound, and the dead will be raised incorruptible, and we shall be changed" (1 Corinthians 15:52). One thing is for sure: We had better be ready for that day.

God's work will continue, no matter what may come. All those evolutionists and other off-brand thinkers must wake up to the fact that God is God, and nothing is going to change that. As I continue to struggle emotionally and psychologically, I also struggle theologically about aspects that I cannot change. I am trying to make the world a better place to live and function as a Christian. Not everyone will accept Christ and live a life for him. Who am I kidding? Every church has members who are lost, like kittens in the dark. Folks, Christ Jesus wants a thriving relationship with us, and it starts when we acknowledge him as Lord and Savior of our lives. What God really wants us to do is totally surrender our complete being to him. Once a person does this, things in life will never be the same. You have Jesus to hold your hand and hear your every thought in life. Better still, you will live eternally in heaven with Jesus. Our small finite brains, which are limited, cannot comprehend that thought. Yes, God's work will continue, with or without us in the picture.

As I have journeyed through these lonesome valleys filled with days and months, God has never once left me. He has embraced me and has listened to every need I have voiced. He has answered all of those needs. For this past year, life has been empty, but it has been full to overflowing because of God's compassionate love and care. It seems like only yesterday I was holding Wanda's hand and walking down the beach. I cannot say enough good things about the congregation which I am blessed to serve. They have been so supportive and loving. They have been compassionate, understanding, and generous to me. They have truly loved their pastor through all of his grief and heartache. I will be eternally grateful to them for their support while I was struggling to get back on my feet. Black Creek Baptist Church family has definitely embraced their pastor in his readjustment to a new life. I will not completely heal, but with God's continued help I will readjust to life in a new way. That new life certainly includes the love and compassion of almighty God.

One must think of our small furry friends and their feelings. I have a miniature pincher who is full of himself. A few days after everyone left the house, I was alone and could not hear Chip running and playing. I sneaked around the corner and looked for him. He was lying on the sofa with his little paws crossed, and he was crying. Yes, crying. I have been told that animals do not know much. You cannot convince me of that. Chip was grieving that his Mama was not to be seen anywhere.

I could not believe my eyes. We both sat together and cried for a while. He is much better now and runs, jumps, and frolics all over the place. I suppose that we both are making it each day, one day after another. Chip is wonderful company and brings a great deal of joy to me.

After all is said and done, as I look back at my life, I can say that I had a wonderful life, with the love of my life. Wanda will never be forgotten as long as I live. I cannot wait to see her when I get to heaven. Life will never be as it was before. I have wonderful memories, but life will never be the same.

I planned another beach trip in October 2016, although Wanda would not be with me. I took my mother-in-law, Phyllis, with me to our favorite resort. We did not need to be in solitude during this difficult time. This was a time for us to regroup and reflect, which would help us to go forward in life. Wanda would want us to go back to her favorite place at the beach and soak in the beautiful sunrise in the eastern sky. Without her in our lives, life will never be the same.

I would be remiss if I did not include the secret of how I was able to continue in this new life of being alone. It is found in the Holy Bible, which is the only piece of literature where we find abundant love and assurance in this life and the life to come. In Romans 10:9–12, these words are stated that offer eternal hope:

> that if you confess with your mouth the Lord Jesus and believe in your heart that God has raised Him from the dead, you will be saved. For with the heart one believes unto righteousness, and with the mouth confession is made unto salvation. For the Scripture says, "Whoever believes on Him will not be put to shame." For there is no distinction between Jew and Greek, for the same Lord over all is rich to all who call upon Him.

These are the words that helped me find the Savior of my soul; I have never regretted saying them, believing or practicing them. Many people look for the keys to a victorious life but never find them. These words bring victory to every believer of Jesus Christ. I assure you that Jesus will make all the difference in your heart, soul, and life. Believe you me: Jesus Christ really makes the difference.

After reading my heart and soul, many of you can resonate with me concerning the issues I have shared. If learning about my struggles have helped you to readjust and have given you a glimmer of hope; I want to ask you to do one thing? Please pass this book along to someone who you think it will help. May God always surround you with his love and presence throughout your lives. Pastor "Boots", a Native American in North Dakota said to me one day while leaving his reservation; "Brother Bill, if I don't see you here or there, I'll see you in the air." All I can say to that is Amen. I also hope to see you one day in the air; I know I will see pastor "Boots."

Made in the USA
Lexington, KY
29 March 2017